The Ultimate Improv Book

A complete guide to comedy improvisation

Edward J. Nevraumont
Nicholas P. Hanson

with additional material by Kurt Smeaton

TD.
Colorado Springs, Colorado

Meriwether Publishing Ltd., Publisher
PO Box 7710
Colorado Springs, CO 80933-7710

Editor: Theodore O. Zapel
Typesetting: Sue Trinko
Cover design: Janice Melvin

Library of Congress Cataloging-in-Publication Data

Nevraumont, Edward J., 1975-
    The ultimate improv book : a complete guide to comedy improvisation / Edward J. Nevraumont and Nicholas P. Hanson, with additional material from Kurt Smeaton.
        p. cm.
    Includes bibliographical references.
    ISBN 1-56608-075-4 (pbk.)
        1. Stand-up comedy. 2. Improvisation (Acting)   I. Hanson, Nicholas P., 1978- II. Smeaton, Kurt, 1977- III. Title.

PN1969.C65 N49 2001
792.7'028--dc21

                                                                2001051396
                                                                    CIP

            1   2   3   4   01   02   03

Preface

Welcome to the world of improvisation. Improv is a dynamic and energetic art form which is expanding rapidly as children, adolescents, and adults are all drawn to the infectious fun and manic laughter that improv creates.

The authors of *The Ultimate Improv Book* have worked toward the goal of making successful and rewarding improv more accessible to people with absolutely no background in this energetic activity. *The Ultimate Improv Book* traces out a path of improv improvement and helps build the skills necessary to evolve as a solid improv performer.

The Ultimate Improv Book is of specific use to drama educators seeking to add improv to their curriculum or to form a team of students interested in competition or performance. People involved in theatre may find improv techniques and theories a great companion to traditional plays and theatre activities. Improv has a broad appeal in many non-arts areas as well. Improvisation can be used for therapy, team building, or learning any academic subject. Quite simply, improv can make people better.

Improv is a creative art and as such there are no strict "rules." But while there are a million right ways to do things, there are also wrong ways. When an individual attempts to learn improv without a structure to fall back on, he/she will usually fall upon one of the "wrong" ways. This manual details a path that will lead to improvisational success, but it is by no means the only way. The best improv to be done has not been included in this manual because it has not been thought of yet. We challenge you to learn our "rules" of improv and to really understand why they work the way they do. When that has been accomplished, the next challenge is to throw away this book and break the rules. It is only by really understanding material that you can effectively go beyond it.

This manual has been a labor of love for the authors. It is our hope that it brings to your lives some of the joy that improv has brought to ours. Learn it well, and then tell us how you made it better.

Edward J. Nevraumont
Nicholas P. Hanson
Kurt Smeaton

You can contact any of us by e-mail at:
improvshow@yahoo.com

Contents

Part One
Introduction

Part One - Introduction

Welcome to the beginning of the meat of this text. This section exists to help someone who has never encountered improv before to develop a platform upon which to build. Chapter One begins with a brief overview of what improv is all about. Chapter Two describes the process of putting together a performance group — what to look for, what to avoid, and how to find these things. Most of the specialized terms are defined the first time they are used. For convenience a glossary has been included in the appendix to avoid any confusion.

Read on and take the first step into the world of improvisation.

Chapter One

What Is Improv?

What is improv?

Improv, short for improvisation, is a form of theatre which does not use a script or predetermined ideas for dialog, direction, or movement. Improv players, usually on a cooperative team, ask an audience for suggestions about the characters, style, location, and circumstances of a scene. The audience gives ideas, and the players, with little or no preparation, spontaneously create an entertaining scene. The players are not falling back on set scripts, nor are they using "tricks" to fool the audience into believing that the scene is being created on the spot. The players are actually making it up as they go along.

Making it up as they go along?
That sounds hard! Is it?

Audiences are consistently amazed and dumbfounded at the scenes instantly created by improv teams. In actuality, anyone can become a solid improviser, as long as they maintain a positive attitude, have the desire to improvise, and challenge themselves to improve their skills.

If improv is all made up spontaneously,
then why practice?

Improv players are always asked this question by non-improvisers. The answer is simple: Becoming a good improviser, like becoming a good anything, takes practice. It is easy to play a sport for fun, but to do it well takes practice. The same holds true for improv. Practice helps a player learn new skills and develop the abilities necessary to create instant scenes. Practice allows players to refine their skills so that they will consistently perform exceptionally in shows.

Why would anyone want to do improv?

People involve themselves in improv for an infinite number of reasons. In a word, improv is fun. Tons of fun. An improv practice or performance is entertaining, energetic, and exciting. As seventeen-year-old player Hank says, "I had more fun in one year of improv than I did in ten years of competitive sports and traditional theatre." Because improv is always different, students, especially those who find repetitive tasks dull, are drawn into this unique activity.

Improv is a perfect activity for people passionate about performance but uninspired by plays or musicals. Friendship is another motivation for improvisers. Improv players live by the motto "cooperate with others, compete with yourself." Lasting friendships are often created between improvisers who are overcome with joy when they discover dozens of people with the same interests as themselves.

Improv is a team activity. Success of a team takes harmony and cohesion between players. Improv fosters interpersonal communication skills as everyone must listen to and respect each other for scenes to work.

What do people get out of improv?

At first glance, improv is a wacky theatre event — do players get anything out of it? Absolutely. Confidence skyrockets. Virtually all players improve their assertiveness. Creativity and problem-solving are increased, as is public speaking, poise, and skill. It is no surprise then that an extraordinarily high number of people successful in education, law, business, and the arts acknowledge participating in improv as an enormous influence upon their lives.

An interesting side benefit of improvisation is the improvement it causes in areas of a student's life. Players quickly learn that anything they do in their life can be applied to improvisation. If they have a grounding in English literature they can use it in a scene. If they know how to sing they can use that too. If they know their current events they have an excellent tap for humor. Students who work in improvisation quickly learn that *learning* is important. They begin going to classes wanting to learn new things, because they have discovered that they can apply these things in a real and direct way. Inevitably this leads to better marks, but more importantly, an interest has been developed in learning which will last a lifetime.

How is this manual set up?

This manual can look intimidating when it is first picked up. There is a lot of material in here. Some earlier attempts to teach improvisation have often been vague and nonspecific. The intent of this manual is to provide a system which, if it is followed through one step at a time, will allow someone who has never before seen improvisation to grow into an expert. The methods in this manual have been tested with groups of children, teenagers, and adults who had never done improvisation before. With ten hours of mass instruction and five hours in a small group setting, they were able to put on a very entertaining show.

Do not try to decipher all of the material at once. Start by reading through the skills section. If you are working with a group, go to the lesson plans and teach the skills in the order suggested. When you are comfortable with these, read through the games and see what catches your eye. Spend a lot of time practicing your skills by playing these games. Eventually move on to the concept of structuring. It is here you will find tips on how to create your own games to play and how to prepare for an improv show.

The manual has been set up so that if you are interested in learning the theory you can read it straight through. All of the helpful tidbits necessary for teaching the skills have been included in appendices at the back of the book.

Chapter Two

Creating an Improv Team

Why improvise in teams?

Many people look at Robin Williams and see a great improviser. It has been said that many of his lines and scenes in his movies involved a camera that just kept rolling while he kept on talking. Individually, Mr. Williams is an improviser of the highest caliber. The skills involved in team improv are a little different. A team must work together to create a scene. There are few people as talented as Mr. Williams who can hold an audience's attention without any outside aid. By working on a team a group of players can create scenes far more entertaining than any one of them could create on their own.

What does an improv team do?

While an improv team might be formed by a group interested in developing their skills in a comfortable setting, improv teams are usually formed with one of two goals in mind — to participate in competitions or to perform in shows.

Who picks the people on the team?

The composition of the team depends entirely on the situation. In a school setting, a teacher acting as a coach would probably organize auditions from the student population. Failing that, an eager improviser may try to recruit contacts to form their own team. Another possibility is that outside opinions be consulted. In the case of tryouts or auditions, the coach might assemble a panel to help assess talent, commitment, and interest. Ultimately, the person who is coaching or captaining the team should make the final decision.

What makes a good improv team?

Eligibility

All participants must legitimately be able to fulfill the conditions of the team. A team competing in high school competitions would not be permitted to have adults play. The professional or amateur status of actors may also come into play in certain situations.

Numbers

A very talented group of performers could do a club-style show with three or four people. For student or novice teams, more improvisers would be necessary — six to eight would be appropriate. More than eight players can be unwieldy to rehearse with and can make performances too chaotic. If a team is performing for money, then the fewer the people the greater the individual cut. In general, all things being equal, the more players the better, but setting an ideal number is impossible. If a team is entered in a competition which allows up to eight players, it is better for a team to play with seven dedicated players than with eight if the eighth is uncommitted, disruptive, or foolish.

Teamwork

As the old sports adage goes, "There's no 'i' in team." Players must totally believe in the ability of the group and must make every attempt to further the group's success, not their own. Players who are optimistic motivators in rehearsal are extremely valuable to a team. Everyone on a team must respect everyone else, not only as fellow players but also as individuals. People who show off are disastrous for improv teams. Even if a person possesses unbelievable improv talent, they can only detract from a team's success if they incessantly hog the focus of the scene.

Ability

Having dedicated, competitive players is important, but people with improv talent are crucial to a team's success. Any group of enthusiastic improvisers can succeed with hard work and practice, but teams filled with charismatic, naturally witty performers who have also worked hard are bound to be more entertaining. Some people are blessed with hypnotic storytelling ability and are captivating entertainers. The rare player with a strong work ethic, firm commitment to the team, and truckloads of ability will form the foundation of any team.

Diversity

Having a team of players with identical strengths, weaknesses, and abilities defeats the point of having a team. A good team should be a well-rounded, balanced, and multifaceted group of individuals. A team would benefit from a mix of reliable and consistent players, vibrant and energetic people, captivating storytellers, imaginative dreamers, solid character players, slapstick personalities, and so on.

A solid improv team has players with different backgrounds. A team with males and females would probably be more workable than an entirely male or female team. Players of different ages will also bring a combination of maturity levels and contrasting perspectives. An important consideration for a team in high school might be having staggered ages which would help to guarantee continued success by avoiding having an entire team graduate simultaneously.

Uniqueness

Improv is such a spontaneous art form that players never have any idea of what to expect. Suppose a scene took place in a dance studio; would it not be convenient to have a ballerina on the team? Special abilities, especially musically oriented ones, can be invaluable for teams. Gymnastics, juggling, impressions, or magic/illusions are all great skills to have. Having a player with "expertise" in a bizarre field, such as Shakespearean sonnets, can be exploited with great success.

How should players be found?

There are a number of ways to create an improv team. People interested in forming a team should select a method (or a portion of one) that best suits their selection.

Recruiting

A person with a decent level of improv ability might decide to contact a few similarly skilled improvisers and assemble a team. This method guarantees quality of participants (assuming that the organizer has worked with all the people in artistic activity previously). This method excludes the chance of discovering a new talent.

Auditions

For people in the community who do not have the necessary improv friends or for any setting requiring equity and opportunity (such as education), auditions are a great way to create an improv team.

When founding as opposed to continuing an improv team, those auditioning are not likely to know much, if anything, about improv. The first job then, before auditions, is to educate people on improv. Sell it, hype it, excite people about being on an improv team. One of the best ways to encourage improv involvement in a high school is to spend a few minutes in each classroom talking. A sign-up list is another good way to gauge the amount of interest. For places with a tradition of successful improv, the often overwhelming interest sometimes requires dividing the applicants into smaller, more manageable, groups.

What should be done with the group?

A different number of approaches exists for what to do during these first sessions.

Interview

Candidates could meet with the selection panel to discuss improv. A brief interview can assess a person's motivation to be on an improv team and the level of commitment that they will offer. Confidence and speaking poise can be readily observed from even a short talk.

Monologs

Candidates might be asked to prepare a brief monolog or two for solo presentation. While a prepared monolog gives no indication of spontaneous improv, it is a display of acting ability and characterization. Anyone willing to invest the effort to prepare a piece for an audition demonstrates serious interest. For more challenge, these monologs could be improvised. (The players are asked to perform a monolog based on a situation given to them at the rehearsal. See the game "Character Monologs" in the Appendix for more information.)

Test

An informal test could be given verbally to a candidate. Questions ranging from silly topics to academic subjects to current events highlight a person's knowledge. If questions are asked rapid-fire, even if the questions are as basic as "what letter follows 'f'?," then a person's reactions under pressure can be seen.

Warm-ups

Play fun games with a large group. A lot can be determined while watching someone play a seemingly meaningless game.

Teaching of skills

Most of the candidates will have had no previous experience; a quick improv lesson on the basics can assess who can pick things up quickly and who cannot. Playing basic games like "Yes and ... " (see Appendix) and others can also show a player's ability to perform.

Play games in small groups

If the group is large it could be broken down into smaller sub-groups which allows the players to play the games simultaneously. Another possibility is to have the groups perform for each other (and the coach) one at a time.

What should the selection panel be looking for?

First of all, the raw ability of players must be considered. Who is obviously talented? Who shines no matter what role they play in a game? Players who learn the skills quickly and improve from their mistakes are invaluable.

The chemistry between certain players should also be considered. Do some players work amazingly off each other? Do some players isolate others and only work solo? A player's work ethic should be carefully examined. The person who slacks during practice is the same person who slacks during rehearsal and performances. Likewise, people who give their whole effort even in silly warm-ups are generally hard workers.

How long till the team is picked?

The team could be picked right away. If there was not an enormous number of people applying, and if a clear division exists between those players who are desired and those who are not, picking the team right away may be a good option. If time is tight and the team wants (or needs) to get practicing right away, then picking the team right away may be the only option.

Call-backs could be in order if the selection panel has trimmed the number to a smaller group (say fifteen to twenty) but cannot decide on the top players. A second audition session could be run much like the first one or could use one of the different options discussed above. Presumably the players will be of a higher caliber than those of the initial practice, so more challenging activities could be attempted. This also allows the selection panel to examine the talent of the remaining players more closely.

Instead of attempting a full cut, the selection panel may choose to keep all of the original number who they feel have a fair shot of making the team. The team would then practice for a while (anywhere from a few practices to a few months) with this larger group. Cuts could be made at any time it is felt that a person is not working out, either lacking talent or motivation. As well, after this period of time, chemistry between people should be readily apparent, and it will be obvious who are really committed.

Part Two
Improv Skills

Part Two - Improv Skills

Anyone can learn how to be a good improviser. While it cannot be denied that talent factors into the success of a performer, a skilled improviser will get much further than one who relies on pure ability. Often talented players will let their natural ability get in the way of skill development. Those who are not naturally funny but learn the skills well will (and do) become excellent entertainers. By following the plan for skill development beginning with **Improv Foundations**, anyone, even those without some special "gift," can become entertaining and exciting to watch.

A number of foundation ideas exist in improv — players should challenge themselves to learn how to be a fundamentally solid players, rather than looking for techniques which might "trick" an audience or teammates into believing that a player possesses more skill than might be true. The terms and ideas introduced in this part will be referred to throughout the manual, so the reader should be sure to be comfortable with them before moving on.

Chapter Three
Improv Foundations

This chapter introduces players to the ideas and theories of improvisational theatre. Working through the sections in order is probably helpful as many of the later concepts build on the ideas of the first few points. Note that not every idea can be learned in an hour. Indeed, for some players, learning the fundamentals can be a lengthy process. Over the course of the rehearsal season, players and coaches should constantly scrutinize themselves to ensure that lessons are being learned.

Can talented players skip the foundations and go on to the other skills?

Absolutely not! Often, some players enter into improv training and discover that they are "naturally talented" and assume that instruction is in no way helpful. Nothing could be further from the truth. While "naturally talented" people exist, any player, *phenomenally talented or not*, who fails to learn and understand the basic ideas of improv will end up frustrating teammates and disappointing audiences. Learn these "rules" well.

Accept everything

Improv is based on the spontaneous creation of ideas. For a scene to be entertaining and exciting, players must accept all new ideas presented by their teammates, the audience, and themselves. Failure to accept new ideas in improv is often referred to as "blocking," which is effectively the killing of an idea. The most obvious method of blocking new ideas is by saying the word "no." When a player says "no," that player is stopping someone else's idea from adding a new twist to the improvised scene.

Here is an example of a player (Lisa) flagrantly blocking a teammate (Joe):

15

JOE: Let's go dancing!
LISA: No.
JOE: All right, let's go to the movies then.
LISA: No.
JOE: OK, I got this great book ...
LISA: No.

Obviously this scene is going nowhere. Blocking occurs so often because players find themselves comfortable in their starting situation, and the acceptance of new ideas forces players to abandon their realm of comfort and jump into a new, unpredictable predicament in which the player is unaware (and thus afraid) of the events to come. Players must realize that real entertainment can only be created once new elements are introduced into the scene and that these new elements are introduced by accepting all new ideas. In the example with Joe and Lisa, if instead of saying "no," Lisa said "yes," the scene would have moved forward and something exciting would have happened.

Saying the word "no" is not the only way a player can block a new idea. Examine Vahid's responses to Betty's comments:

BETTY: I have some shrimp for you like you asked.
VAHID: I wanted salmon.
BETTY: (*NOT* blocking) Oh yes, salmon, and with it your favorite wine.
VAHID: I don't like wine.
BETTY: (Trying her best) In that case, this fine glass of ice water.
VAHID: I am not thirsty.

In this example, all of the action is generated by Betty, who is trying her hardest to create a new idea which is acceptable to Vahid, who is killing all of Betty's ideas in a more indirect method than simply stating "no." Many players act like Vahid; that is, they are too picky and selective with what they choose to accept. Perhaps Vahid wanted Betty to offer him a job or perhaps Vahid simply disliked Betty's ideas for no clear reason. In any case, Vahid should have accepted Betty's first offer of shrimp, because players should always accept everything. Potentially, Betty had an incredible idea for a scene based on shrimp; when Vahid failed to accept her offer, that incredible idea was wasted. Additionally, Betty, like any team player, expects her teammates to accept her offer. When Vahid did not, he forced Betty to scramble to create another new idea in a very short period of time. Keep in mind that players have no way to communicate with each other when they are on-stage beyond what is observed by the audience.

Not only must players accept their teammates ideas, they have to accept their own as well. Consider Mike's failure to accept his own suggestion:

> MIKE: We should build a fire.
> SARAH: (Accepting) OK, let's do it.
> MIKE: Actually, I'm warm enough.

In this case, Mike offered a new idea to Sarah, who accepted it eagerly. Immediately afterward Mike blocked his own idea by stating an opposite view. If a player creates a new idea, they must ensure that they remain consistent and accept the new idea's existence.

Players must also accept a new idea in a full and complete manner. Consider Will's half acceptance of Mary's statement:

> MARY: You appear to be moving your arms like a bird flaps
> its wings.
> WILL: I'm just limbering up. I get sore after I work out.

Mary's comment to Will involved two elements: "arm movements" and "birds." Will had an infinite number of ways to accept Mary's statement involving both elements — maybe Will is a bird in disguise on a mission to kidnap human beings; maybe Will is in love with birds and wants to be one; maybe Will is a former airplane pilot who lost his plane and now wants to fly himself; or maybe Will is in training to be Batman's sidekick Robin. A number of possibilities for acceptance existed, but each of these possibilities forced Will to enter the world of the unknown. Instead of leaping forward by accepting the whole idea, Will opted to only half accept the idea of Mary's. (He accepted the "arm movements" but failed to accept the "bird" aspect.)

Note that blocking ideas is often funny. Outright rejection of other people's ideas is the basis for a number of comedians and comedic styles. Criticizing or "shooting down" is used frequently in sketch comedy and in sitcoms. Performers in plays have scripts, so they know where the action will go after the rejection; on the other hand, the improviser has no safety net, and blocking in scenes causes long, awkward responses." Failure to accept a new idea may create entertainment for the moment, but it slows down and unnecessarily complicates the scene, negatively affecting it in the long run.

Players must ensure that they are accepting every new idea. A talented improviser who is not concentrating can accidentally fail to accept a new idea. Players must remain alert.

Blocking stops things from happening, and since making things happen is what improv is all about, players should accept everything. Things are guaranteed to happen.

Hold on to ideas throughout the scene.

Once players are aware of the accepting, they must also learn that once a new idea is accepted, it must be accepted for the duration of the scene. In the world of improv, once a new idea is presented and accepted, it becomes a law that must be respected without exception. Watch the way Tom handles Megan's idea:

> MEGAN: Is there a doctor in the house?
> TOM: I am!
> MEGAN: I cut my leg and I need you to sew it up!
> TOM: Well, I'm not really a doctor. I just like to tell people that I am to impress them.

In this case, Tom originally accepted his role as a doctor and then later reneged and denied being a doctor. While Tom's last line might make people laugh, it does nothing to further the scene. Once Tom said he was a doctor, he should have stuck with being a doctor for the rest of the scene. Making Tom a doctor for the whole scene does not limit Tom's imagination — Tom could have been an incompetent doctor, an evil doctor, a veterinarian, a doctor of English, etc. Any of these options would have provided levity while maintaining the reality of Tom being a doctor.

Players must ensure acceptance of physical ideas as well. Suppose Ted is miming that he is driving a car. If Sally walked right in front of him and said "hi" in a happy manner, then she failed to accept the car's existence. If Sally walked in front of the car, she should have dived out of the way and yelled "Crazy driver!," or she should have fallen down screaming in pain as if she were hit by the car. Now suppose Tom parks his car. If Sally walks up behind Ted and pokes him in the back, then she has again failed to accept the physical characteristics of the car (a car is so many meters wide and long, etc.).

Players should also realize that accepting the permanence of ideas does not lead to stagnancy. Suppose Zed is faced with a dilemma: He needs a big jar, but the only big jar around is filled with cookies. This notion of continued acceptance of ideas does not mean that the jar has to stay filled with cookies. Zed could somehow get the cookies out of the jar, as long as he did it in a logical manner. Instead of failing to accept the permanence of the situation with "Wow! Suddenly all the cookies disappeared!," Zed could solve his problem by eating all the cookies in the jar. Note that eating all the cookies would have consequences — Zed might feel ill, for example.

In order to avoid inadvertently and carelessly failing to accept previously accepted ideas, a player must ensure that they are paying attention to what their teammates (as well as they themselves) are presenting in the scene.

Always look for the bright side!

Once a player is comfortable with the concept of accepting everything, they should learn how to accept new ideas in a positive manner. Consider Stavros' response to Andy's question:

ANDY: How was the movie?
STAVROS: It kind of sucked. I didn't like it.

In this example, Stavros has accepted Andy's new idea, but she has drained the energy of the scene. When a player is faced with a

19

choice on how to accept a new idea, in general the player should make it a positive one. If one player begins a scene by spray painting a wall, another player entering as a police officer should comment on the amazing artistry of the graffiti, rather than criticizing him for poor use of color.

Being positive is scary. Players often possess a natural tendency to act in a negative manner, because it shields them from risk. Being positive is important to improv because it makes vibrant and entertaining scenes. When Stavros said the movie "kind of sucked," she kept herself safe by failing to commit to an opinion. If Stavros said, "It was the best movie ever made. It changed my life. Nothing could ever be better!," she would have made the scene exciting and interesting, but increased her own personal risk. What if Andy had responded, "I would not have thought a movie about snails could have been that good?" The scene would grow more interesting, all because Stavros entered into unknown territory — something which is hard to do. Taking the effort to make positive ideas happen is the mark of a player overcoming an inborn handicap to avoid risk.

Keep it moving!

Tell, don't ask

A good player moves the scene forward and does not rely on someone else to do it for him. Suppose a team is comprised of a pair of veteran improv players and a handful of novices. The new players might be inclined to sit back and watch the veterans guide the scene. All of the players must believe in themselves and contribute new ideas for a scene to be of exceptional caliber.

In this example, consider the role of Mel:

> JEFF: Oh my gosh that thing is big!
> MEL: Yeah! It's really huge!
> JEFF: It's getting bigger!
> MEL: It sure is!
> JEFF: My goodness it's eating my dog!
> MEL: The poor dog!

Mel has accepted all of Jeff's ideas (i.e., she did not block), so did she perform brilliant improv? No, because she has done nothing for the scene itself. Improv is about sharing, and it is everyone's shared responsibility to push the scene forward. What Mel did in this example (accepting an idea [i.e., not blocking], but not adding to it), is often referred to in improv as "wimping."

The most common form of wimping is asking questions. Watch how Perry accepts all of George's ideas, but then wimps by simply asking questions instead of contributing new ideas.

> GEORGE: Look at the new dog I got.
> PERRY: What breed is it?
> GEORGE: It's a German Shepherd. It can protect me against people.
> PERRY: Who do you need protection from?
> GEORGE: The Mafia. They are out to get me.
> PERRY: Why?

In this scene, Perry forced George to create all the ideas. Improv works far better when the workload is shared.

> GEORGE: Look at the new dog I got.
> PERRY: Wow! A German Shepherd. You must need protection.
> GEORGE: Yeah, the Mafia is after me.
> PERRY: I told you not to date that girl.

See how much faster and exciting the scene is. Both players are working together to create an interesting scene. Perry stopped asking questions and started making statements. Eliminating questions and redundant statements allows improv teams to pack more material into their scenes.

In the top example, one player was improvising successfully and the other was wimping. Sometimes there are instances when neither player is willing to advance the scene — a double wimp. This impasse of decision making, with both players unwilling to define anything, is often called "waffling." Instead of making a decision, even when *any* decision will suffice, everyone avoids making a decision of any kind.

21

Imagine a player opening a box to find a gift:

EMILY: Look what I got.
ALASTAIR: It's very nice.
EMILY: Yes. And big.
ALASTAIR: It is certainly bright.
EMILY: Bright indeed.

A scene like this collapses, because both players are afraid to take *responsibility*. Many novice players are concerned, "What if the scene does not work out? It will be my fault." Worrying about success is a dangerous way of thinking in improv. While it is true that a scene might not work, lack of certainty is one of the things that makes improv so exciting! Players who believe that wimping and waffling will prevent them from embarrassing themselves discover that their scenes will never be interesting.

Waffling occurs because no player wants to be personally responsible for the failure of a scene. When presented with an option, making a decision, *any* decision, will help a scene. Failure to make a decision delays the action, and the longer the delay, the harder it becomes to define what is going on. In the example with the opening of the gift box, it would have been easy for Alastair to say "Wow, a miniature car!," "Wow, an icicle," "Wow, a deck of cards" or any number of things; however, by the time the waffling was done, the thing in the box had to be something that was nice and big and bright. Once players begin waffling, the scene often falls into a downward spiral because both players become more and more tempted to continue waffling.

Wimping and waffling are very common at the beginning of scenes. Instead of jumping in and starting something, players wait and delay. Each player keeps waiting for someone else to do something, which can create an excruciatingly uncomfortable pause.

The following is an example of a nightmare, worst-case scenario of waffling:

HARRY: Hi.
JILL: Hello there.

HARRY: So whatcha doing?
JILL: Nothing much. You?
HARRY: I don't know.

This conversation bears resemblance to an awkward conversation from real life, such as a relationship breakup. We have all had these conversations in real life, but chances are they were not fun then, and they are definitely not fun to watch on-stage.

Use body movement and physical action

If players accept all new ideas, tell instead of ask, and make decisions, a scene could still look like this:

AMIRI: We should go to the store.
PETE: Yeah! We could go and buy those clothes you always wanted.
AMIRI: For sure! Plaid is so in this time of year.
PETE: And what with you being an undercover cop and all ...
AMIRI: All the underworld is wearing plaid these days.

The scene is moving forward and both Pete and Amiri are building on each other's ideas, but nothing is actually happening because words are replacing potentially exciting actions. This form of spoken scene is often labeled as a "talking heads" scene, because the bodies of the players are not being used. The audience hears about these actions instead of getting to see them being enacted. The scene would be far more interesting to watch if Amiri and Pete were actually shopping in the store. Perhaps they could run into one of the underworld people and he wants to know why Amiri is not wearing plaid. Outlandish banter between players is often funny, but it pales in comparison to the enjoyment of watching players physically enact wacky predicaments.

Don't delay!

If you got it, use it

Many players will think of a good idea at the beginning of a scene. Instead of using that idea as soon as they can, they drag out the scene, "saving" their good idea. The player stalls from adding anything to the scene because they feel that they should use their funny idea as the scene's climax. Unfortunately, the scene drags while the audience watches and waits for something to happen. Of course, nothing will happen until the player who has been stalling the whole time unveils his "brilliantly funny ending idea," which is used on an audience who has grown uninterested watching dull improv.

The following is a clear example of a scene with a player (the boy) who is clearly postponing the use of his idea:

BOY: I like you ...
GIRL: I know, I like you too.
BOY: But, well, I have to tell you something.
GIRL: Wow! You're going to ask me to marry you.
BOY: Well, not exactly, you see ...
GIRL: What is it?
BOY: Well, um, you see ... Have you seen the new movie?

And so on. The player playing the boy is afraid to say "I want to break up with you" because he does not know what comes next. In an effort to play it safe and to save his "good idea" (breaking up with the girl), he says meaningless things. The player should have started the scene with the breakup and let the scene develop from that point onward. The scene could continue in any number of directions, and the fact that neither the audience nor the players know exactly where it is going makes the scene come alive.

Head to new directions

A player may delay the scene by repeating the same actions or words over and over. Suppose Jack is having his feet tickled by Barbara, who is playing the part of an invisible person. If Barbara continues to tickle Jack's knees and arms and nose, then moves on to other parts of his body, the scene is not being advanced. Comedy might exist as the audience is amused by the continued antics of Barbara, but eventually once the joke has been exploited, the audience will be frustrated if the tickling continues for an extended period. Barbara should head the scene in a new, unexplored direction: make noises, move the furniture, or interact with other players. Heading to new directions is a very important concept for narrators or players making long speeches. Speakers must ensure that they do not repeat material and that new ideas are continually explored.

Relate everything with logical connections

When new ideas are injected into a scene, they must be clearly related to everything else already existing in the story. The audience should be able to observe the logical intersections of the different ideas. Teams should note that "logical intersections" does not mean that scenes must be tedious or normal — rather, actions must be justified within the context of a scene. Suppose a team was performing a scene about stealing a TV from inside a house. If a hoard of elephants ran into the house, the audience is left wondering "where did the elephants come from?" because there is no relationship between the elephants and the theft of the TV. If one of the the players stealing the TV mentioned, "Hurry up guys, Tarzan is going to come home soon" or "Hey, this is a funny commercial advertising peanuts," then the arrival of the elephants is more understandable. (They arrived to avenge the theft of Tarzan's TV or they were attracted to the peanut commercial.)

An apparently unrelated idea can be used successfully if the team reincorporates the idea, providing clever justification later on in the scene. The ability to use an idea in this manner is a more advanced skill, used effectively by players with solid storytelling backgrounds.

Make it make sense

New ideas created by a player must fit into the internal consistency of the scene. Rationality must exist when a player builds a scene forward. Players who try for laughs will probably invent extreme but illogical events. After witnessing the oddities, the audience is left thinking, "What was that?" or saying, "That was dumb."

Imagine an improviser shaking dust out of a carpet. A player looking for bizarre ideas might:
- get hit by lightning

- be attacked by a dog
- be swallowed by a whale
- meet a famous person.

All of these actions were wild and wacky, but have nothing to do with the carpet. A more focused improviser, who makes their actions make sense in the context of the scene, might:

- discover it is a flying carpet
- get into an argument with the fleas that lived in the carpet for kicking them out of their house
- tie the carpet to his neck and become a super hero
- get dust on his face so that he is not recognized by his friends.

Notice that these ideas stay within the consistency of the scene. Notice also that these ideas are still wacky and wild, but they are far more effective because they make sense.

Up the stakes!

Players should search for ways to increase tension and maximize trouble in every scene. Adding complications to an already problematic dilemma is a wonderful source of entertainment. Watch the way Alicia "upped the stakes" in the following:

HARRY: Oops! I just broke my mom's vase.

ALICIA: That vase was a gift from your mom's great-great-great grandmother.

Harry's breaking of a vase would probably get him into trouble with his parents. When Alicia added that the vase is immensely important, she increased the tension — Harry's mom will not be mad but furious. Harry will try extra hard to somehow replace or fix the vase before his mom finds out because he is so afraid of the consequences.

Good improvisers make their characters get into worse and worse trouble as the scene progresses. When good improvisers break up with their boy/girlfriend, they find out they need a date to the prom later that night. Good players break things when they keep house for other people. They lose the ring on the way to the wedding. They run out of antiseptic in the operating room. They mistake their boss for their underling. In any situation, players should not let themselves, or their teammates, get off easy.

Stay within the mood

Players should make sure that all their words and actions fit into the mood and tone of the scene. If performing a serious or sincere scene, the players should not be clamoring for laughs. Even in humorous scenes, players should refrain from making excessive jokes that will take away from the scene and lose the story's base. Watch how Frank and Tim deal with an issue:

FRANK: You said you were helping my sister with her math homework, but you were really trying to pick her up.

TIM: Listen Frank, you're my best friend ...

FRANK: You are right; I've *added* this up and there is definitely a *division*.

TIM: Are you *integrating all the factors?*

FRANK: I think I got to the *root* of this and I am going to *subtract* you from the conversation.

While this scene might be amusing, it has turned the issue into a pun-fest. All interest in the story has been lost. The audience no longer cares about the relationships between the friends and the sister. One-liners are funny only in moderation and only at appropriate times. Making the audience fall apart in laughter is counter-productive if it is done at the same point another player is revealing important elements of the story. Teams who make constant jokes endanger themselves, because if the new jokes are less funny or less frequent than previous jokes, then the team is left with neither comedy nor a stable base. If the audience cares about the story, players do not have to be as funny as often. (This is why sitcoms create relationships between their characters so that the viewers will stay interested beyond and between the gags.)

Build it up

Scenes must begin with a platform — a basic premise for the

27

scene. Players should continually increase the amount of tension in a scene, adding new characters, problems, and story elements. Players must ensure that they advance the scene at a moderate pace — throwing numerous and drastic dilemmas all at the same time into the scene leads to chaos. When an idea is completely explored, then a new idea should be introduced. A scene has a better chance to succeed if it starts with a stable platform and has the stakes raised than if it starts out with high stakes and has nowhere to go.

Making offers

The key to a good improv scene is making good offers and having them successfully accepted. All of the ideas listed above are different methods used by players to make offers and accept them. On its most basic level, scenes are a series of offers and acceptances. Players should keep this idea in mind throughout scenes to emphasize the importance of making and accepting offers.

One important type of offer is the blind offer. In a blind offer the player making the offer does not know in what direction the scene is heading. They make an offer of "something" and let a teammate interpret it as they choose. For example, a player may start a short vignette by saying, "My, it sure is damp." This player may have no idea at all where to proceed. They count on the other players on their team to accept that "blind offer" and build on it. The next player may say any number of things:

- "You're right. The dome is leaking. Atlantis is ruined!"
- "Don't worry, it never rains on prom night ... "
- "I don't care if it's damp. You are going to mow the lawn anyway!"

Each statement gives a million possibilities of where to go next. If players understand the need to move a scene forward, the humor will come. It doesn't matter in which direction they're going, as long as they are going somewhere.

A blind offer can be even more open-ended. Consider Todd's actions:

TODD: Here, Chris (Holds his hands open to CHRIS.)
CHRIS: Golf clubs! Perfect! Just what I always wanted!

In this scene, Todd did not say, "Here are some golf clubs," nor did he mime an object that could only have been golf clubs. Rather, Todd trusted the abilities of his teammate and created an opportunity for Chris to create a new idea for the scene. Blind offers are effective, because instead of having players force the scene in a certain direction, the scene must be opened up and subjected to the combined creativity of the team.

Chapter Four
Rules of the Stage

Before the team goes further with their improvisation skills, they should be comfortable operating on a stage. Basic theatre conventions and presentation are essential for a good improv scene. Just as a comedian would not think of telling a joke without working on his delivery, an improviser should think of the rules of the stage when they are performing improv.

Work on these skills should begin early in the season and should be spread out over the course of the year. The players should keep the rules in the back of their minds when they are developing other skills in the manual. Eventually the skills will come naturally.

Rule #1: Think about the voice

If a player cannot be heard, they cannot be entertaining. Voice skills can be divided into two important aspects:

Make it clear

Just because a player knows what they are saying does not mean everyone else does. They should avoid mumbling like the plague! (And *definitely* take out the gum, candy, etc.) It is of the utmost importance that the audience is able to understand what is being said. The speech should be enunciated. Improvisers should concentrate on the words they are saying and make sure they come out clearly. People having problems should slow down their speech. There is a natural tendency, especially when nervous, to speak too fast — very seldom do people speak too slowly.

Make it project

Chances are high that the team practices in a drama room, basement, or small, empty space. In a small room, it is fairly easy to be heard. When the team performs, it will probably be in a theatre or club. These can be quite large, and it is necessary that everyone can hear from the front row to the back corner. (They all paid the same price to see the show.) Speaking loudly and clearly can be challenging. Yelling is not effective; this is a common misconception that will lead to the demise of voices before the night is through. Voice projection involves producing a noise that sounds normal but is louder than usual. The human body uses the diaphragm not the throat to force out the air. Even stage whispers can be done by speaking in a huskier voice to give the illusion of whispering while still being loud enough for the patron sitting in the corner.

Rule #2: Think about the body

Not only does the audience want to hear improv players, but they also want to see them. Improv is extremely physical. Players should direct the body toward the audience and keep it there. Ninety percent of the time the audience should see a player's entire face (called "mugging the audience"). The ten percent of the time when they do not see the entire face is only when the players are in intimate conversation with someone else in the scene. In these instances the audience should still be able to see *over half of the face.* Traditional theatre also follows this convention of keeping faces pointed at the audience and often refers to it as "cheating."

In normal conversation people face the person they are talking to. In theatre, actors also have to make allowances for the audience, so the difference is split. If a player is at a forty-five-degree angle with the front of the stage, they can talk to their fellow players in the scene and still be seen full on by most of the audience. It may not seem natural at first, but it is something that every player has to get used to. Unless there is a very specific artistic reason (for instance an abstract style being presented), or the theatre space is a thrust or arena stage, players should avoid turning their backs to audience members."

Rule #3: Think about the stage

When a player enters a theatre, the stage can be intimidating. The stage is big, the audience is big, and problems can be big if players are not prepared for them. Using the entire stage effectively is the sign of a great team. It's convenient to divide the problem into four components:

(a) Pay attention to the other players

No one should ever stand in front of other team members. This is known as "physical blocking" (very different than the blocking discussed in the last chapter). If another player is in front, the rear player should move to the side and make themselves seen. They should work together as a team. Sometimes the problem gets more complicated than this. If Derek is downstage center and Rita begins a conversation with him from upstage left, Derek has to turn away from the audience to see what she is doing and to talk to her. Derek now has his *back to the audience.* The audience cannot see or hear him properly. He has "upstaged" himself. Any time a player directs his attention or focus towards the back of the stage he has upstaged himself, which is something that should be avoided.

(b) Play down on the stage

The closer the team plays to the audience, the better. Something amusing at the rear of the stage is downright hilarious at the front of the stage. Players look like they are more confident and in control (even if they are not) and the audience appreciates them more. Teams that play at the back of the stage (upstage) look like they are scared to be there. Everyone gets nervous, but the teams that play at the back of the stage *look* like they are nervous. The teams that play at the front of the stage look like nothing could scare them. Playing downstage has the added bonus that players can be seen (think about the body) and heard (think about the voice). Notice how the rules begin to overlap.

(c) Use the whole stage

Players have a huge stage to work with, so they better use it. It is easy for a team to bunch up and only use a tiny section of the stage. Good teams move around and utilize all of the space they are given. The main focus should be kept in the front (play downstage), but actions should happen in the background, on the sides, or even in the audience. Sometimes this movement of the team is referred to as "working the stage." In rehearsals, spreading out should be stressed. If the team is ever bunched up, the scene should be stopped and they should be spread out again. Bunching can make a scene boring to look at and make it harder to create fluent stage action.

(d) Balance the stage

Once the team has grasped the idea of playing downstage and using the whole stage, they can begin to work on balancing out the stage. This means that they do not have an uneven number of players in one part of the stage. It is aesthetically pleasing to have a symmetrical stage to look at. In scripted theatre, this happens through the carefully choreographed action. In improv this has to be done by having players who keep their heads up and watch what everyone else on their team is doing.

Rule #4: Think about levels

We live in a three-dimensional world. After a team has mastered the art of horizontal stage work they should begin to think about height. The more players are positioned at different heights on-stage the more appealing the scene is to look at. Having a team member stand on a box while another is kneeling and a third is lying on the ground can create some interesting visual action. The symmetry and balance that were created should not be lost, but height is an important consideration when players are positioned on the stage.

The earlier rules should always be kept in mind. A smaller object should never be behind a bigger one. Everyone should be kept visible and well spread out at all times. Levels are an excellent addition to an improv reservoir, but never forget the basics.

Rule #5: Think about confidence

This should not be confused with characters who are confident. Rules #5 involves a player's confidence as an actor. It is normal for anyone to be nervous when on-stage, but overcoming it is essential. Confidence helps overcome the nervousness. Confidence gives a stage presence to which an audience is drawn. Performing within the parameters detailed in this chapter will give a player an aura of competence which will help build up their stage ego. Confident players are not afraid to try new things on-stage. While insecure players are looking at the ground and playing far upstage, confident players are loud and clear. Insecure players are the ones who have their hands in their pockets and speak quietly or hushed.

It is OK for a player to be nervous and scared when they are on-stage, but they must put on an illusion for the audience. The best way to enhance confidence is to learn and know the basics of improv and trust other teammates. As skill increases, so too will confidence on-stage. If a player does not think they are confident, they can pretend. If they keep their head up, stay downstage, and speak loudly, they can "trick" the audience into thinking they are confident. In the end, it makes the player actually become confident. It works.

Summary

Here is a quick list of things a player should think about when they are on-stage:

- Be loud. Project your voice. Don't yell.
- Face the audience. Keep your front to the audience. Keep your face visible. "Cheat."
- Pay attention to your teammates. Don't block each other. Make sure everyone is visible.
- Play downstage. Don't clump on one part of the stage. Balance the stage.
- Use multiple levels whenever possible. Put small objects/players in front of big ones.
- Be confident or at least *look* confident. Lie to the audience.

Chapter Five

Who? What? Where?

By now, the improv group should be familiar with the basic concepts and ideas of improvisation. They should be able to go on-stage with confidence and be seen and heard. They can accept offers from their teammates and move scenes forward by avoiding delaying and wimping. Now they are ready to begin creating improvised scenes. Scenes should begin where all stories begin.

What are the important questions?

All stories (and improv scenes are stories) are built out of six key questions: What? Who? Where? How? When? and Why? If a scene answers these questions effectively it will have created something which is interesting and entertaining.

Which of the questions is the most important?

Teams should concentrate on the first three (what, who, and where). These questions tell us the main points of the scene.

The what

The **what** is the action of a scene. It is the plot of the story or the information the players are presenting. Answering this question tells everyone **what** happens.

Consider the example of *Jack and the Beanstalk*. In this fairy tale, **what** would be: Jack trades in his cow. Jack plants the seed. Jack climbs the beanstalk. Jack steals the golden goose. The giant chases Jack down the beanstalk, etc. The **what** is the story that you are telling.

The who

The **who** consists of all the characters in your scene. Characters are people but they can also be animals, vegetation, or even inanimate objects. The **who** carry out the action of the story. They are the ones who affect and are affected by the **what**.

In our example of *Jack and the Beanstalk*, the **who** are: Jack, his mother, a cow, a bean salesperson, the golden goose, and the giant. (In some versions of the story you could also include the beanstalk and the beans, etc.) If a rock is thrown, it is an object. If a rock is upset that it is being thrown, it is a **who**.

The where

The **where** consists of the location or locations in which the scene takes place. In an improv scene the location can be physicalized (see Chapter Six) and/or mimed. The **where** also includes less conspicuous details. New York in 1810 is a different **where** than New York in 2025, so time is a component to the **where**. A **where** should also involve such things as temperature, atmosphere, smells, light, and textures.

Jack travels through a variety of **wheres**: a poor farm, a path along the way to the market, Jack's home, a beanstalk, and a giant's palace. In all of these **wheres**, the time period is the middle ages and magical things can happen.

What about the other questions?

The last three questions ask for details which help explore the first three questions.

The when

The **when** is not the time period of your scene. That is part of the **where**. The **when** is related to the conflict in the scene. Does the scene take place after, during, or before the conflict? Where does the scene fit relative to the **what**?

In Jack's story we are telling the full **when**. We begin with Jack trading in the cow and end with his escape from the giant. Remember that things have happened before our "start" and will continue to happen after our "end." We pick the **when** that our story takes place in. In doing so we take the most interesting part and show it to the audience. Jack's story could easily be told beginning with his climb up the beanstalk. In some short improvisation, players may wish to cut a scene short in such a manner.

The why

The **why** is the most difficult and most ignored of the questions. The why consists of the reasons behind the **what**. Why do things happen in your scene? Everything in the world happens for a reason. The following are invalid answers to the question *why*. *"Because it's improv!"* *"Because that's what the suggestion is!"* *"Because it doesn't matter!"* It **does** matter! Not using **why** makes for dull and unconnected improv. Anyone can have random events occur for no reason. Things should always happen for a reason in a group's scenes.

Using the example, the **what** can be explained with the **whys**: Jack goes to sell the cow because they need money. Jack trades the cow for beans because the salesperson makes them irresistible. He steals the golden goose because he needs the gold, and so on. There are purposes for every event in the story. At no point does something happen without a reason.

We can include under the concept of "why" the question "where did that come from?" We can accept that Jack cuts down the beanstalk with an ax. An ax can certainly be found in the environment we have described for him and he would use the ax to chop wood anyway. We could not accept Jack cutting down the beanstalk using lasers from his eyes. It does not make sense and would not be **consistent** with the realm of the story. Jack has never had such powers. A scene can be fantastical and magical, but its events, characters, and objects must be explainable.

An example:

"The Jeep is on fire and I can't pull over!"

"I have a bucket of water."

Where did the water come from? Perhaps this would be better:

"The Jeep is on fire and I can't pull over!"

"I'll use the car phone to call a fire truck. Hello? We're on Highway 7 and our Jeep's on fire. Thank you. They'll catch up any minute."

While the solution was perhaps silly or far-fetched, it came from the environment and was plausible. The audience will accept something crazy if it makes sense.

The how

The **how** deals with the manner or method in which the **what** is presented. The **how** is often a genre or style, but not always. It is how the story is being told or how the information is being presented. Every **how** has specific elements which make it unique. (For more on the how, see Chapter 18 on structuring **how** games.)

In Jack's story the **how** is a fairy tale.

What does this have to do with improvising a scene?

We have broken down the story of *Jack and the Beanstalk* into six questions. The answers to these questions are what makes the story what it is. These answers make the story unique. By changing the answers to two or three or even four of the questions or sub-questions, teams could radically change the scene. Imagine substituting Jack with Mr. Potatohead (who). Picture the scene set in a future barbershop (where). What might it look like as a musical (how)? Think about how these changes affect what the story is like. How is the story different? How is it the same?

These six questions are variables from which any scene can be created. The reason why one scene is different from another flows from how the performers answer each one of these questions. When improvisers begin asking for suggestions from the audience, it will be these variables that they are asking for. For now the questions should be kept in the back of the mind as teams move through and look at the other skills needed to create an improvised scene.

Chapter Six

Physicalization — The "Where"

Improv is usually presented in a normal theatre — black floors, black walls, etc. Despite this fact, the audiences can be treated to watching vibrant scenes and crazy things. This happens with physicalization. Physicalization is the technique used by improv players to create imaginary locations, objects, and events.

The goal of physicalization is to make the audience "see" something. The entertainment level of a scene is greatly increased when the audience gets to watch exciting activity on the stage. It's better to have an entertaining scene in a barber shop (or an airport or a living room or *anywhere*) than to have a scene in empty space.

How can a player create something?

Use their body

A player can use his/her body to create an object. If done effectively, the audience is easily convinced and amused by the creation of such objects. A player could stoop on their hands and knees and pretend to be a coffee table. A player could place their hands over their heads and be a tree.

Use blocks or props

You may have props available to you that can be used in scenes. Many stages have black wooden blocks, tables, or stools that can be used any number of ways. The easiest way to use these items are as pieces of furniture, but they are not limited to that single use. A block can be used as a pop can, a cannon, a hat, or a squirt gun. Players can let their creativity run wild.

Use mime

A player could create an object using mime. Instead of using body parts or the blocks to "create" the object, the player could pretend to interact with space as if it were an actual object. For example, an improviser might hold their hands apart as if they were manipulating a chainsaw.

How can players make sure physicalization is effective?

Do not ruin what has already been created

If a player mimes a table and gives the table dimensions, ensure that the table is not walked through. This respect of physical existence requires the entire team to pay attention to the actions made by all players, so that no one cancels the creation of others.

Do not be vague

When creating an object, ensure that it is not an ambiguous form. This is another form of delaying as discussed in Chapter Three. Evaluate the object that is being created and consider what its unique qualities are. Make an attempt to incorporate the unique qualities when creating an object. For example, a weathervane has four directional pointers and it spins in the direction of the wind.

Keep in mind the length of the scene

While the action in a scene may fly by, time will drag on (sometimes painfully so) if a player attempts to create objects by placing themselves in uncomfortable positions. For example, placing their hands straight up in the air or doing a handstand may prove to be physically uncomfortable for the duration of even a one-minute scene.

Do not be afraid to change

If a player is physicalizing as an object and the scene changes direction and they feel like they could make a positive contribution, it is acceptable to stop being the object and become something else. For example, if they are acting as a coffee table and another player on the team comments that someone should be knocking on the door soon, it is acceptable (and valuable) for that player to stop being the coffee table and jump into the role of the person at the door.

Chapter Seven

Characterization — The "Who"

For most of the scenes a team performs on-stage they will not be playing themselves. They must create captivating characters to use in the scenes. The audience will become engaged if they are given these interesting characters to watch. When someone acts in a play, they often have months to prepare how their character walks, talks, and carries themselves. In improv all of these choices have to be made very quickly. As is common in improv, it is more important that these choices be made than what the actual choices are.

How well developed do the characters have to be?

For the purposes of this manual we are assuming teams are performing in short (approximately two- to six-minute) scenes. In this limited time frame there is not a lot of room for extended character development. It is important that strong choices are made early on in the scenes. Imprinting characters with a predominate character trait will often make the choices easier. If a "mantra" of a distinctive attitude is kept in mind throughout a performance, it will create a foundation for any character developed.

The more extreme the character, the easier it is to play and the more entertaining they will be for the audience. If a character is sad, they should be extremely sad. It could be interesting to see that they are sad their dog is dead, but it gets even more interesting when the audience discovers they are also sad when they stub their toe. A competitive character should not only try to win at football but should also compete to see who can eat the most, who can blink the most times, and who can tie their shoes the fastest. They should try to win things that other people do not even care about. An improviser playing the role of someone smart should be the smartest person who ever lived. When players only have a limited time to create and reveal their characters, extremes are the preferred option.

What is the focus?

There are a number of areas characterization can focus on. All of them should be explored during the duration of a performance.

The entrance

From the moment a player enters the stage, the audience should know that they are playing a distinct character. The first thing the player should think about is how their character walks. A lazy person walks quite differently than a brave person. The character's walk and entrance onto the stage are the first impressions the audience has, so it is important that they are good ones.

Players should think of the different walks they have seen throughout their lives. When they are on the street they can be looking around and evaluating the different ways people walk. If they take those differences and exaggerate them, they have created an interesting character walk. The lazy shuffling of the feet walk becomes more pronounced. The excitable character starts to really jump and bounce. Often the distinct walk and entrance will get a laugh before the player even speaks. In fact, it is best if the character is explored physically before they verbalize their traits.

A character who says they are scared is not nearly as entertaining as a character who cowers when they walk.

The first words

After the character has been explored physically, improvisers can have them begin speeking. In the beginning, less emphasis should be placed on what the character says and more on how they say it. Players should create voices for their characters different than their own. Some will be easy — a whiny voice or valley-girl voice, for example. Others will take a little more effort — how would a hypocritical person talk? How about a cool character? There are many options on how to interpret a character so the key is to have players make a choice and stick to it.

With the voice comes the mannerisms. Hand movements and the way a character stands should supplement their voice. Generally this physical side of a character will come naturally when an improviser changes the way they are speaking. It is not

42

necessary (nor desirable) to spend a lot of time concentrating on exactly how hands will be moved. Instead, the player should let go and let their body do what it wants to do. When a player starts speaking in character, the rest of the body will follow. The important thing is to let it. Players sometimes become self-conscious and are afraid to give up themselves and become the character. They need to let themselves go.

What they talk about

If a player has truly created a character with their body and their voice, the verbalizations of the character should not be hard. If players try to "think" of things to say related to their character they will often get stuck and run out of things to talk about. If instead improvisers "let the character do the talking," they do not really have to think at all. When people talk to their friends, most of the time they do not have to struggle to find the next thing to say. After a player has fallen into the character role they are playing, the same phenomenon should take place. If the player just talks, elements related to their character should come out.

How they talk about it

No two characters will see the same thing the same way. If an artistic character were to describe this book, they might say that it is "a marvelous collection of prose which speaks to the heart and lets the soul transpire to become greater. The words flow through the parchment like water through a brook, bringing awe upon those who glance directly at its pages." An intellectual character might describe it a little differently: "A series of rectangular surfaces (approximately $8^1/_2$ by 11 inches) which contain knowledge that could be assimilated through the reading of said material. The words in question consist of English grammar and pertain to the art of improvisation."

Throughout the scene the character should be kept in mind and players should be thinking of their reactions to the events around them. They should play extreme characters. Audience members do not want to see normal; they see it every day. They want to see the exceptions to the rules, and it is up to the team to give them that.

Chapter Eight

Storytelling — The "What"

Many improv scenes will involve a story in some form. But what makes a good story? How can novice improvisers learn to tell a good story "on the fly," improv-style?

Good stories are not always funny, but it is hard to be funny without telling a good story. If players concentrate on telling a good story, the humor will come. But if they spend all their time searching for jokes, they will not obtain a good story, and odds are they will not even be that funny. People will laugh more if they care. (Stand-up comics know this — how many times do comics discuss their personal lives?) Improvisers have a responsibility to make the audience care by telling a good story.

Most stories have three sections which must be constructed effectively in order for the story to make sense.

Start at the beginning

Stories need a starting point. If the characters jump right into the conflict at the very start of a scene, the audience will feel no connection to the characters. Any outside observer cares about the story only as much as they care about the characters in the story. Hamlet would not be as gripping if it started with Hamlet's battle with his stepfather. Generations of filmgoers would not care if the boy gets the girl unless the boy, and hopefully the girl, too, are people who have shared their experiences. Many beginner improvisers, in an effort to have instant action, make the mistake of skipping the beginnings of their stories.

The beginnings also offer a nice, easy place to develop ideas. In improv, the entire story idea does not need to have been scripted out in advance. Many an improviser has said, "I do not have an idea." This is just not true. Starting the story with the beginning is the first step. It is an easy first step that anyone can do. Let us list off some beginnings:

- A girl is talking on the phone to her friend.
- A man is digging a ditch.
- A dog is playing with its owner in a park.
- An astronaut is in training.
- A woman is going for a run.
- A messenger is being given an important package.

What do all of these "beginnings" have in common? They all involve someone doing something in a safe, stable environment.

So, to start a scene, all an improviser has to do is do something (anything) that does not involve conflict. Take the goodies to Grandma's house, build a house out of straw or maybe send up a hot air balloon. Any normal, non-threatening action can be the beginning of a story.

In improv terminology, these non-threatening actions are called "routines" or "platforms." These routines should continue until they establish the *where* and the *who*. The action itself exists as the *what* for the moment, and the *why* can remain a mystery (see the Ws in Chapter Five for more information on these terms).

Isn't watching a non-threatening routine boring? No. The audience will be drawn into any routine action improvisers perform at the beginning of the scene. Only if nothing comes of it will the audience be disappointed. Players do not want their routine to be boring, and by *physicalizing* and exploring the platform it will not be. The audience will trust that this is just the beginning and that something will happen. When that something does happen, the team can move on to the next part of the story.

Proceed to the middle

By beginning the scene with a routine, teams have made a promise to the audience. If the improvisers keep that promise, the audience will appreciate the platform that the team has set up for them. If the players break their promise the audience will be disappointed. Consider these two scenes:

Both scenes start with a player digging a hole in the ground with a shovel.

45

Scene 1

As the man dug the hole he heard a noise. He left the hole to travel on a large journey through the wilderness. There he met many strange creatures and had incredible adventures. He found a woman with whom he fell in love. She became his wife and they lived happily ever after.

Scene 2

As the man dug the hole he heard a noise. His shovel had hit a buried chest. He opened it up exclaiming that this was what he was looking for. Upon opening the chest he got sucked into another world where he met many strange creatures and had incredible adventures. He found a woman with whom he fell in love. She became his wife and they lived happily ever after.

Both of these scenes are very similar, but they have one important difference. One keeps its promise, but the other does not. Which scene creates a satisfying (if somewhat short) story? Which example leaves an aftertaste of being puzzled or cheated?

For the beginning platform to work, it needs to be incorporated into the rest of the story. This is referred to as "breaking the routine." There are an infinite number of ways to break a routine, but they all must *relate* to the routine. For example, reconsider the example of the man digging the hole. How could that routine (digging the hole) be broken?

- Earthworms start talking to him.
- A policeman arrives to accuse him of grave robbing.
- He finds buried treasure.
- He hits China.
- The hole caves in and he becomes trapped up to his head.
- His shovel gets stuck.

All of these examples of breaking the routine involve the act of digging the hole. They are all things that could be in the mind of a member of the audience. This is very closely related to "making it make sense" which was discussed in Chapter Three. If players break the routine by doing something unrelated to the activity, they have broken their pledge to the audience. The improvisers might as well have not set up the routine to begin with.

So the first two steps in telling a story are:
1. Set up a routine or platform in a non-threatening environment, and
2. Break that routine in some way related to the routine itself.

Now what? There has to be more to a story than that. There is.

Expand upon the middle

The middle is the meat of the story and needs to be expanded upon. The middle fills the most time in the story and makes or breaks the story. Many players get stuck there. Learning to start routines is not difficult. Learning to break those routines is a little harder, but coming up with what comes next seems even more intimidating. Do not worry; there is a trick for this, too.

Whenever players break routines, they end up creating new routines. For example, consider the routine breakers from our shoveling example:

- Earthworms start talking to him.
  The routine is talking to an earthworm.
- A policeman arrives to accuse him of grave robbing.
  The routine is dealing with a policeman.
- He finds buried treasure.
  The routine is opening the treasure chest.
- He hits China.
  The routine is exploring China.
- The hole caves in and he becomes trapped up to his head.
  The routine is trying to escape the hole (maybe yelling for help).
- His shovel gets stuck.
  The routine is trying to free the shovel.

Each time an improviser breaks a routine, they set up a new one — automatically. It is just a matter of realizing what the new routine is. In order to keep the story going, all a team has to do is keep breaking routines over and over again. The first time a team fails to break a routine, they break the promise of logical connections.

There is one more step required to finish the middle.

47

Bring back the beginning

Effective storytelling always brings back the beginning or some other part of the middle. This technique is known as "reincorporation." Anything that players draw attention to at one part of the story needs to be brought back later in the story. Consider a murder mystery. If the detective finds a clue, that clue needs to be important in the search for the murderer. Perhaps the clue helps find the killer, or maybe it was a red herring and sends the investigators on the wrong track. It does not matter how it affects the story, just that it does. It would be very disappointing indeed if they just ignored the clue altogether. Too often this is what happens in improvised stories, because players are working so hard to develop new ideas that they frequently forget to expand and explore all of their old ones. Reincorporation, when used effectively, can be enormously popular with the audience, who are delighted to see a further exploration of one of their favorite aspects of the story.

Writers of plays and books have an advantage over improvisers in the creation of coherent tales. An author writing a story could go back and eliminate things that were not reincorporated or revived. For example, the writer can decide that the clue dropped at the beginning was not that important and did not contribute anything to the plot; easily, the clue could be eliminated from the story by deleting it from the page before it is ever printed and given to the public, who would be unaware of the previous existence of the clue. Improvisers do not have that luxury.

This example will illustrate a story that involves the making and breaking of routines (comments in *italic*).

- Joe was writing a book on his computer. *(Routine)*
- The regular beat of his fingers hitting the kegs made him drowsy. *(Breaking the routine)*
- He began to drift off to sleep. *(Starting new routine)*
- He dreamed of far-off lands with dragons and wizards. *(Breaking routine and starting new one)*
- Someone shook him and he woke up. *(Breaking routine)*
- His wife told him they were going out. *(Still part of the broken routine)*

- He began getting dressed to go out. *(New routine)*
  (At this point it would be easy to begin hedging and break the dressing routine. Really, the routine is going out, so any breaking of the dressing routine is really delaying going out.)
- They go out and have a fabulous dinner together. *(The end)*

Something still feels wrong about this story. There was no *point*. There was no reason anything happened. It was just a series of unrelated routines that were broken one after another. To tell a real story, it is necessary to link the routines together and to reincorporate. Let's try again:

- Joe was writing a book on his computer. *(Routine)*
- The regular beat of his fingers hitting the kegs made him drowsy. *(Breaking the routine)*
- He began to drift off to sleep. *(Starting new routine)*
- He dreamed of far-off lands with dragons and wizards. *(Breaking routine and starting new one)*
- Someone shook him and he woke up. *(Breaking routine)*
- His computer is talking to him. *(Reincorporates the computer; starts a new routine)*
- His computer complains that he wants the massage to continue. *(Reincorporates the hitting of keys)*
- Joe starts typing again. *(New routine)*
- The computer thinks the story that Joe is writing is *stupid*. *(Breaks routine; new routine)*
- Joe changes the story to be about dragons and wizards. *(Reincorporates dream; breaks routine)*

This time the story is satisfying. By bringing back old ideas, the story begins to have a point.

Anytime a player brings back something from earlier in the story, they will get a cheer from the audience. An audience might grow irritated if the team spent all its time bringing back old components and never creating anything new, but in moderation the reintroduction of old ideas is great. Anytime players get stuck and are not sure how they are going to break a routine, they can think back to what happened earlier in the scene and reapply it to the present.

Ideally everything introduced in a scene will be reincorporated at a later time. In the story above, we do not know *what* Joe was writing, *how* the computer was talking, or *why* the wizards and dragons were important. All of these things should be explained and brought back before the scene ends. Every mystery should be solved.

Build to a climax

A good story will keep building these routines and reincorporations to a greater and greater level of importance (raising the stakes, discussed in Chapter Three). These will build until they hit a climax (otherwise known as the highest stakes in the story). Where the climax will be depends on the story. If it is a story about feeding your hamster, maybe the climax is the hamster escaping and running around the house. If it is a story about an evil rodent genius, maybe the story starts with the hamster running around the house and climaxes with a battle to save the world. The choices and the routines of the team directly influence the occurrence of the climax. The key to captivating storytelling is to never let one "routine break" be at a lower level of importance than one that came before it. If the scene's stakes keep rising and the tension keeps building to an exciting climax, the story will be entertaining.

Bring it to an end

When the team has solved all of the mysteries and has created and linked together all of the routines, the story is finished. It should be fairly obvious when the story is done — all the suspense and tension has dissipated and all conflicts are resolved. It usually helps to reincorporate the beginning after you finish the climax (i.e., " ... and so they traveled back to the castle and ruled the kingdom peacefully for many years"). If the team leaves something hanging, the audience may be disappointed ("whatever happened to that rabbit?"), but if the team reincorporated everything, then the story should be a satisfying one.

Note: Take a look at the games in Chapter Seventeen, "What" Structures, for other advanced ways to tell stories.

Chapter Nine

The Huddle — Before You Begin

What is a huddle?

If an improv team is taking suggestions from the audience, they usually allow themselves some time to discuss the suggestions and plan their scene. The planning time is know as the huddle. Some styles of improv allow long huddles (up to half an hour), and others allow no huddle at all. This chapter is concerned with a more recommended, short huddle (five to forty-five seconds) to plan the scene. This brief amount of time does not annoy the audience with a long wait before the scene and allows the scene to be created without a lot of pre-planning. Working on the huddle is key for teams as it also teaches excellent teamwork skills. An effective huddle is the sign of a quality team.

What happens in a huddle?

Half a minute or so is not a long period of time, and an efficient use of this time is critical to the creation of a strong scene. The audience's suggestions will trigger a number of ideas in each improv player's head. The main goal of the huddle is to sift through these ideas, select the ideas most conducive to the creation of a good scene, and agree on a plan for the scene. Generally, the huddle is used to decide on the five Ws, *who* on the team will play which characters, *where* the scene will take place, *when* the scene will take place, *what* actions will take place, and *why* these actions will take place.

Consensus is a key theme of the huddle

The huddle does not provide an adequate amount of time to fully debate the merits and flaws of each player's ideas. Thus, decisions must be made which are agreeable to everyone. Every player should exit the huddle with a clear sense of comprehension about the scene that is about to be created. While the original thoughts and ideas may transform over the scene, each player should be aware of the intended plan.

How can a team make the huddle work?

The sense of panic created by the challenge of improv, coupled with the nervousness of being on-stage, makes many players lose their focus. Chaos in the huddle is a frequent problem for teams, and an alleviation of the disorder is usually beneficial. There are a number of methods to instill some sense of order in the huddle.

Break it down

Assign a single role or idea for each player to create. If a team is attempting to tell a story based on an occupation, an object, and a location, instead of forcing all the players to think about the situation as a whole, break it down into parts and have each player concentrate on one (or maybe two) specific components of the scene. For example, in this scene, the team asked for an occupation, an object, and a location. Let's suppose that the audience gave the football team coach (occupation), a block of butter (object), and a bank machine (location). In the huddle, Sheila concentrates on qualities of the occupation: Football coaches know a lot about sports, are tough, talk with a loud voice, have a whistle, etc. Cynthia concentrates on qualities of the location: Bank machines have electric-opening doors, video surveillance, beeping noises, etc. Bert concentrates on qualities of the object: Butter is a food, very fatty in content, melts easily, etc. Eric concentrates on a connection between the occupation and the location: The coach was going to the bank machine to withdraw money to bribe a referee in an upcoming game. Sharon creates a problem: The coach did not have any money in his account, so he tried putting his hand into the machine and it got stuck. Jose creates a solution to the problem: The coach blows his whistle in an attempt to summon help; a dairy farmer answers his call, uses a stick of butter to grease the coach's arm, and pulls it out of the machine. Thus, instead of having each player waste the huddle by being overwhelmed with panic, this method allows each player to concentrate on a more narrow topic, usually with successful results.

Decide the end

Some teams benefit in deciding during the huddle how the scene will end. The desired goal is for each player to make decisions during the scene which are compatible with the eventual outcome and thereby compatible with the decisions of the rest of the team.

Decide the start

Conversely, some teams find that deciding the outcome constricts their creativity during the scene. These teams prefer to decide on the beginning ideas and continue with them, wherever they may lead.

How can the huddle be improved?

The four-minute huddle

Try creating scenes with a four-minute huddle. Once the team is using the time effectively, allow two minutes of planning time. After the team is comfortable with this stage, reduce planning time to one minute. Next, reduce the amount of time in the huddle to forty-five seconds. Then the team gets thirty seconds. Once the team is working well with that time, cut the huddle to fifteen seconds. Teams looking for a greater challenge can then pare the huddle down to five or ten seconds.

Huddle without scenes

Have the team practice the huddle without actually performing the scenes. This method allows teams to use a fifteen-minute period of time to practice dozens of huddles, which would take hours if the team was presenting each scene in full. For example, the team is preparing for this scenario: "Your neighbors go on a vacation and ask you to watch their house. You host a massive party and the house is destroyed. They return home seconds after the last guest leaves." In whatever length of huddle the team plans on using, the team decides to present a scene taking place in the living room of the house, with Fernando playing the role of the party organizer who explains to the house owners that a giant tornado hit the house, resulting in massive damages. Rather than present the scene, the team moves on and is faced with another suggestion and another huddle.

Chapter Ten

Teamwork

Improv is a team activity. The very idea that started this section (accepting offers) tells us that improvisation is only effective when a group works together as a team. In most sports, a team of average players with years of experience together will do better than a bunch of exceptional players thrown together. The same holds true for improvisers. Clearly the whole of the team is far greater than the sum of its parts. Overall, teams benefit most by using the talents of the individual members to their fullest.

What are common teamwork problems?

Several people speaking at the same time

This problem occurs when two or more players insist on pushing their own ideas onto the scene but meet with resistance from other players who have different ideas about the direction of the action. Unfortunately, when several players speak at the same time, no one idea is clearly expressed and the audience is left with a scene that is painful to watch. The problem of speaking over each other can be alleviated with several methods. Teams may create "rules" about speaking for the players. For example, a team may decide that if two people are having a conversation and a third person enters, the third person is entering with a new idea and should be given priority. Additionally, teams may decide that when a person speaks, other players may not begin to speak until the first player pauses for at least one second.

Upstaging and distractions

Many teams suffer from having a player (who is usually a talented comic) hog the audience's attention and try to maintain individual focus for as long as possible. Players who upstage, while sometimes inserting entertainment into the scene, often damage the scene by adding unnecessary or confusing elements. Players need to respect the idea of the team. Performances are not carried on one person's shoulders, and when show-hogs steal the team's attention for themselves, they reduce the caliber of the whole. Upstaging can also occur at the back of the stage. Players who are not satisfied with playing a role in the background will sometimes attempt to steal the attention of the audience. For example, suppose a team is enacting a scene in a cafe. Two players could act as the central action in the scene by engaging in a conversation at the front of the stage. If a third player was to act as a waiter in the background, then he should behave appropriately to the background. Should the waiter mime that he is engaging in a heated argument with another customer and continue miming getting a knife and stabbing the customer relentlessly in an exaggerated manner, then that player is distracting the audience from the conversation between the two players at the front of the stage, which is where the focus of the scene should be.

Listening and watching

Some players spend their time on-stage concentrating on new ideas to contribute. This continual process of ideas is wonderful, but the players must also divert a part of their attention to what is being said and acted by the players currently directing the scene.

If Devon were to say, "Whoops, I just dropped a whole crate of land mines on the floor," then Ben, who had been planning to enter the front of the stage, should not proceed as planned casually walking to the front, thereby canceling the newly created mine field.

Players should always be listening for any way to help contribute to the scene. If Jill says, "Hey, I just heard the door knock," then someone on the team should jump without hesitating to be the person answering the door. It does not matter if the player has no idea why Jill wanted someone to knock on the door. Jumping to answer the door makes for seamless movement and makes the team appear to be very cohesive. Treat these instances like offers that need to be accepted by someone to make the scene move forward.

How can teamwork be used to proactively help scenes?

Most scenes will be performed with two or three main speaking players. The others in the group will help create the where by physicalizing. The focus should, in general, remain on the main players for that particular scene. However, players who are in the background are by no means "out of the loop." In addition to listening and watching for offers given by the main players, they can find new ways to help a scene. The next three methods of teamwork are known as "walk-ons." A player who has been in the background of a scene comes forward and contributes something to a scene and then leaves just as quickly. Many of the funniest and most entertaining moments come from walk-ons since the players have a lot of time to think up something effective to add.

Saving the scene

Improv is a team activity; thus, one person cannot "ruin" a scene. Occasionally, however, an individual may act in a way which is damaging to the quality of the scene. If things go badly, **it is not the fault of the single individual.** Rather than sit idly while the scene is deteriorating, a good team player should jump in and "save" the scene, by injecting a new idea or directing the scene in a more desirable manner. **A good principle in improv is to enter the focus of the stage when the scene is not going well, and to refrain from entering when things are progressing smoothly.**

Feeding a scene

This is an exception to the rule of thumb. A player can enter and feed a scene when the scene is doing well. Feeding can mean one of two things. Its primary use is to "feed" a characteristic. A player does something that shows the characteristic of another player. There are three distinct ways to feed a characteristic. To understand this concept, consider the example of Randy as an extremely happy shop owner and Jess who enters the scene to feed his characteristic:

"Randy, I got this brand new clock for you!"

This lets Randy show his happiness by being excited for the new clock.

Jess can also try something called a reverse feed:

"Randy, I just heard your dog has died ... "

Randy can still show his happiness by being happy about something that most people would find very sad. Perhaps his dog was vicious.

Finally, Jess may enter the scene and show Randy's characteristic without Randy having to do anything at all. A self-contained feed:

"Wow! There sure are a lot of flowers and balloons in this shop!"

Randy appears to be happier (the characteristic has been shown in a new way), and Randy himself did not have to do anything other than let Jess talk for a line or two.

Feeding becomes even more important with some hard-to-show characteristics. There are characteristics that are very hard to present without other people helping you out (miserly or gullible, for example). If Fran is gullible, Mark may come up to her and ask for her wallet. Mark has given Fran the opportunity to show her characteristic by giving him her wallet. Without Mark to help her out, Fran would be hard-pressed to show how gullible she is.

Feeding can be used beyond characteristic suggestions. Any suggestion can be fed in a scene. If the suggestion was "tissue paper" and it was not being used effectively, a player in the background may enter with a runny nose. They have fed the suggestion in a way that only that suggestion could have been fed. See "The Hot Dog Stand" game (page 206) for more information on feeding in a scene.

Raising the stakes

Life should always be getting worse or harder for the protagonist. Whatever they are doing should become more and more important over the course of the scene. Part of that responsibility falls on the character himself (see "Up the stakes!" on page 26). The players in the background also have jobs to do. They can walk on, and by saying only a line or two, raise the stakes of a scene. If AJ is arguing with his girlfriend, Janis, and she is saying that they are not spending enough time together, a background player can "walk on" and say something like, "Hey AJ, we still going to the baseball game on Friday? Great, man." The "walk on" just made things worse for AJ and increased the audience's enjoyment of the scene. See the "Raising the Stakes" game (page 208) for more help on this concept.

Chapter Eleven

Use of Suggestion

Why is use of suggestion important?

There are many stories of people not believing scenes are really improvised. Improvisers can get very good at their craft, often to the point where people sometimes doubt their talent. Audience members will sometimes see what performers are doing and think it is a trick, like magic, or (worse) a well-disguised script. Hopefully no improviser would do this, but how can the audience be convinced that they are not watching a team presenting a pre-made play? The key to true improvisation is to use the suggestions given by the audience.

Use of a scene's suggestion clearly shows the audience that the scene was not planned weeks in advance. If something is done that is funny but does not relate to the suggestion, it could have been pre-planned, whether or not it is irrelevant. No one watching can tell the difference between a scripted scene and an improvised scene that did not use suggestion. When on-stage, improvisers must **prove** that they are improvising at all times. The only way to do this is by **using the suggestion**.

Use of suggestion can work to the advantage of an improviser. Consider the team that performs a freeze game for an audience. They may decide to use it as their warm-up and first game of the night. To make it easy on themselves, they decide not to ask for a suggestion and just play the game. Have they really made it easier for themselves?

If the team practiced the game once before the show (which every team should do something), then it would be very easy for them to do the same scenes they did backstage. What would be stopping them? The audience has not seen that funny "Smurf" sketch they just did, so why not do it again? There are lots of reasons including the fact that it will not help you warm up your improv skills, it will make you lazy performers, and it is just plain unethical to pass off previously performed work as improv.

If the team has more "integrity" for improv than to really cheat (a commonly heard phrase about groups who do not ask for audience suggestions), they are forced to come up with new ideas they did not do in rehearsal. This is fine, but what ideas are they going to use? With a game like this, someone has to start scenes and that involves coming up with ideas. If a player goes out of their way to avoid the good ideas they had before, they are going to run into problems. The first thing that happens is that the players will begin "saving" their good ideas. If someone has a neat idea for a chess board scene, they may not use it in rehearsal, instead "saving" it and surprising the rest of the team in the performance. (How this gives the improv more "integrity" is puzzling; the player still thought of it before but just did not tell anyone.) Second, if they avoid the "saving" of ideas, they are just putting off coming up with ideas until the last minute.

What is the solution?

Imagine that instead of just "performing," the same team asked for a suggestion. They began their freeze game by addressing the audience: "Could we please have an idea or concept that our scene will relate to?" Now all of the scenes will have to relate to that idea. There is no longer any reason to save ideas in rehearsal, because the team did not know what suggestion they were going to receive; they are forced to think up ideas while they are on-stage. Teams no longer have to avoid cheating since cheating becomes impossible. The audience will know anytime they do something pre-planned — they can tell because it would not relate to the suggestion.

Can a team "trick" the audience?

Sometimes teams (or individuals on teams) think they can trick the audience. They "fool" the audience by taking their suggestion and then applying it to something they had pre-planned. Their attitude is: "The audience will think we came up with that idea in our huddle." But they won't.

The audience is not dumb. If they are ignorant about improvisation (and many audiences are) then it is up to the team to educate them. Teams that keep their audiences in the dark and then "trick" them fail in a different way. In addition to doing poor improv (regardless of how funny their "script" is), the ignorant audience will stay that way and fall back on the ideas that "improv is a trick." If a team wants an audience to believe they are doing real improv they must first educate them and second **do real improv!** Uneducated audiences will think teams are tricking them and educated audiences will see through tricks. Either way, they will not be fooled.

So what does all this have to do with the suggestion?

The answer to all of these problems is to use the suggestion. Does that mean teams cannot have any pre-planned elements in their scenes? No. Take a look at Part Three on structuring for more information on how to pre-plan elements effectively. However, if elements are pre-planned, teams should still try not to trick their audience. They should tell the audience the parts they pre-planned. If they decide to do a scene about Batman and Robin, then they should *tell the audience!* They should not ask for a location and an occupation and then try to "trick" the audience into thinking they came up with the idea of putting Batman and Robin in that situation during the huddle. The audience should be told up front. "The next scene you are going to see is a Batman and Robin scene. What we need from you is ..." The audience appreciates the effort. It becomes a lot less tempting to drop in Batman jokes when the audience will **know** they are pre-planned. It makes a team think twice about trying to "fool" the audience. It would not make any sense — the audience has been educated.

How does a team use the suggestion?

Hopefully this manual has spent enough time describing what a team should not do. Now how does one use the suggestion well? The key is to use it as many ways and as much as possible. Virtually everything in the scene should be about the suggestion. When a team asks for something, it should not be used in just one way. If they ask for an animal and get a monkey, they should think of all the ways they can use a monkey in the scene. A player could be a monkey. Someone could slip on a banana. Players could "jump on the bed 'til they hit their heads ... " Tarzan may come looking for Cheeta, his pet monkey. The suggestion becomes used in every unique way possible.

What makes a use of the suggestion unique?

It depends on what was asked for. If a team asks for a vegetable and gets a carrot, the fact that it is a food is not a unique characteristic. Any response from the audience would have been a food. However if they asked for an **object** and got a carrot, the fact that it is a food **is** a unique characteristic. It should be stressed that if something *could* have been pre-planned it might as well have been. The suggestion should be thoroughly explored. If a team asks for a politician, they should not make politician jokes! But if they ask for a famous person and get George Bush, then they can use as much political humor as they choose.

There are "Use of Suggestions" games in the Games Appendix which will help teams improve at finding the unique characteristics of suggestions.

To end the chapter, consider this example. Assume a team asks for an object with which to defeat the villain in an improv story being performed.

Suggestion Given	Poor Use of Suggestion	Good Use of Suggestion
Baseball Bat	Hit him with it.	Have a sidekick throw the villain and then hit a home run.
Umbrella	Hit him with it.	Do a rain dance and protect yourself with the umbrella.
Orange	Throw it at him.	Squirt the orange acid in his eye.
Lamp Shade	Hit him with it.	Put it on his head so he can't see and then turn him off.

A team does not have to think too hard about how they will use a suggestion; they can be obvious and still be very entertaining. Regardless of the other, unique ways the suggestion is used, the most common ways should be stressed. A team that does this well will be loved by their audience.

Chapter Twelve
The Presentation

Improvisation is all about presentation. Material delivered in a fun and exciting way will be entertaining and enjoyable for the audience. The same scripted play can be phenomenal or atrocious depending on its presentation. An improv team with an effective presentation can go a long way towards succeeding on-stage. Teams can develop presentation skills so that even during lags or lapses in the scenes, the audience is entertained.

What if the team is not funny?

In some ways, acting is simply lying to the audience. Players create characters that are not themselves. Players can choose to have the characters that they are playing be funny. A player who convinces himself that he is "not funny" won't be. If an improviser slowly walks on-stage with his head down and wears a face like their life is over, then jokes probably will not be flying. It is up to the player (even if their world is over!) to *lie to the audience!* If he pretends to be happy and cheerful and smiles and looks like he is enjoying himself, then the audience will like him better. Players need to choose to be vibrant and to exhibit their joy.

How does a player build up a punch line?

This method of building humor is showcased in this example of "The Object" game (page 198). Players are given an object and are told that they have to kill themselves with it. If they walk on-stage, do some vague action and die, it is not funny. If they build it up they get a laugh almost every time. The way to build it up is threefold.

- **The setup:** Chris goes onto the stage and uses the object in the way it is normally used. (For example, Chris shaves his face with a razor.) He remembers to choose to be funny.

- **The buildup:** Chris keeps it up, but makes it a little more extreme. Chris begins shaving all the parts of his body. He keeps the same happy attitude.
- **The send-up:** This is the moment before the point of no return. It is the set-up for the joke. Chris pauses. He thinks about shaving his tongue. He sticks out his tongue and looks at the razor.
- **The end:** End it smoothly and efficiently, not necessarily quickly. Chris cuts his tongue. Fake blood spurts out. He acts surprised that he is dying.

Is that it?

No. The presentation and being funny are difficult tasks that involve great amounts of timing and reading of the audience. But it can be learned. Good presentation is not something that people are born with. Some people learn how to do it when they are young and quickly become classified as "funny people" and others who do not learn it early become "not funny." The process continues when the "not funny" people begin to think of themselves as "not funny" and then *choose* to be not funny. Make a conscious choice to be funny.

Chapter Thirteen

One Final Concept

At this point, it can be assumed a team understands all of the skills that go into creating an improvised scene. The next section of the manual helps develop the ability to create polished improvised structures that can be used very effectively in performance. Before going on, let's reiterate what has been taught earlier in this section through the use of a new concept. There is no new material here; it is a slightly different way of thinking about improv ideas. By exploring improvisation in different ways, a greater understanding can be reached.

What is the concept?

Every player in every scene can break down what is happening into three components: the Goal, the Vehicle, and the Obstacle.

The goal is the character's objective. Goals can change throughout the scene.

The vehicle is the means the character (or player) uses to accomplish the goal.

The obstacle is the person, place, or thing that is in the way of the character accomplishing the goal. The obstacle is the source of conflict in the story.

The goal is the desire of the character or player in the scene. Goals are pursued until one of three possible conclusions is reached:

• They are accomplished.
• There is another, more important goal.
• The goal becomes impossible to accomplish.

A goal can take the entire scene to reach a conclusion, or it can take only a few seconds.

In most cases, when the main goal of a character is accomplished, the scene is over. (Teams should concentrate on this idea during vignette games.)

As actors, the players will have slightly different goals. One goal may be to make the scene entertaining or to make sure the scene keeps moving forward. Both the player and the character will obtain their goals through the same vehicle.

In improvisation the vehicle should **always** be the suggestion. The suggestions are the tools the character uses to accomplish their goals. Use of the suggestion as a vehicle is what makes scenes different every time they are played.

How about an example?

Suppose a team has a basic game where they ask the audience for an occupation and a characteristic. Now suppose the audience gives the team "lumberjack" and "conceited." The basic idea of the game is that the characteristic causes a major problem in the workplace of the occupation. By the end of the scene the problem is solved in some way using the characteristic.

The character's goal is to pay attention to him/herself (conceited). The **vehicle** is the suggestion (lumberjack). The player may admire himself in the saw's reflection. He may brag about cutting down trees. He may attempt to be louder than the chainsaw so everyone can hear him.

The actor's goal is to cause a problem at the occupation site and then later to fix it. The **vehicle** to do this is the suggestion. Perhaps the lumberjack, Samir, gives away all of the chainsaws (lumberjack suggestion) because they are taking too much focus away from him (conceited). He can no longer cut down trees, but Samir solves this problem by going to the media (conceited) and bragging about all the good things he is doing making the environmentalists join sides with the lumber company (lumberjack).

If players know what their goal is at the beginning of a scene, both for themselves and for their characters, and they know what the vehicle they will use to obtain these goals is, then everyone knows what they should be doing. There becomes a reason for being on-stage.

Note that when using the ideas of vehicles and goals, the "questions" will always fall into place. The lumberjack (who) gives away the chainsaws (what) because they are making too much noise (why).

It cannot be overstressed that the "why" must be used when the character uses the vehicle to achieve the goal.

One final example

If the suggestions are "barbershop" and "anchor," then it must be answered **why** the character has the anchor in the barbershop. Perhaps the anchor weighs the customers down in the chair and holds them still so the barber can cut the hair. By finding an appropriate why, players use both of the suggestions at once.

Making the connections between the suggestions and the rest of the scene is a huge part of what improvisation is all about.

Part Three
Structuring

Part Three - Structuring

Now that the team has developed the improvisational skills necessary to perform on-stage, it is time to start developing the games they will play. While it is possible to find a number of training exercises in the appendix of this book that will work as performance games, most improvisers will wish to eventually develop a structure of their own. Structures allow a team to present a whole night of improvisation and still have each game look and feel different.

This part divides the types of structures into five categories. Each type of structure focuses on a different aspect of improvisation, although within each concept large differences are possible (which will become obvious shortly).

What are the five categories?

This section focuses on five different concepts for structures, which explore the Who, the What, the How, the Use of the Suggestion, and Reality (or non-comedy-based improvisation).

What exactly is a structure?

A structure is a framework that helps teams create an improvised scene. It is one of the hardest ideas to get across in improvisation. The idea of a structure seems to go against the basic idea of performing improv and not following a script. Finding the right balance of structure and pure improv for a team can be a difficult feat. A framework that is too structured becomes a script that the team follows, sometimes dropping lines here and there relating to their suggestion and frequently making references to events outside the suggestion. A good structure, on the other hand, facilitates use of the suggestion and makes improvising fun and easy while still letting that improvisational magic happen.

A structure is not always something complicated. For example, "The Typewriter Game" (page 221) is a good example of a "what" event. The focus of the game is to tell a story and the way of doing that (the structure) is through the use of a narrator who pretends to be typing on a typewriter.

The Canadian Improv Games

These events follow the same principles as the Canadian Improv Games (C.I.G.) events. Each focus we describe is roughly equivalent to a C.I.G. event. By designing your C.I.G. structures with the principles described here, your games should be effective. We have included an appendix on the C.I.G. events to reveal how these concepts can help you flesh out your games.

Chapter Fourteen

Flags

What are flags?

A flag is an element of a structure which uses the suggestion in some way. Most improv structures move from flag to flag in an organized way. This is best explained with an example: Imagine an improv scene which is to take place in a jail. The team asks for two characteristics for the two people stuck in the jail.

1. The criminals show their characteristics in the jail while interacting with each other. They explain why they are in jail, related to their characteristics.
2. The jailer feeds each of the players in ways related to their characteristics.
3. The two players use elements of the location to show their characteristics: sink, contra-band materials, other prisoners, dirt, etc.
4. At some point during the scene, the criminals take their turns writing letters to their friends outside of jail. While they are writing, off-stage players act as voice-overs, again showing the characteristics.
5. The scene builds to a confrontation between the two players and ends in a flourish (where they may or may not escape the jail).

Read over each of those **flags** again and notice how each one helps the players use their suggestions (the two characteristics) in new and different ways. In this case, the flags were very open and general. Flags can also be much more specific. Some scenes go so far as to flag every line! Note that it is difficult to design a very specific, detailed structure that still uses the suggestions fully. As an example, here is a scene that has many more flags. It is an inspirational learning video in which the team asks for a skill that could be taught:

71

1. A boy is performing the skill.
2. A girl enters and is amazed at his proficiency. She explains how she is good at many things *related* to the skill, but cannot perform the skill.
3. The boy explains that she can learn how to do it, as could anyone.
4. A guitar player enters with an inspirational song. Two players sing four rhyming lines each, related to the skill.
5. Back to the boy, where he explains to the girl that the skill is rather easy. All she has to do is one *basic* thing.
6. Entire team chants that basic thing.
7. Back to girl who explains to boy that she has learned that basic thing but still has problems, and she explains those problems. Boy tells her that she needs an expert.
8. Host interviews an expert on the topic "on location."
9. Back to girl who explains to the boy how well she can do the activity now. The two of them do it together in a big, exciting way.
10. Expert and host summarize "what was learned today."
11. Guitar player enters and ends it with a four-line rhyming couplet.
12. Everyone repeats the last two "catchy" lines a number of times.

Because there are so many flags in this case, each one is relatively quick. But notice that in each one, the suggestion (the skill) is explored more fully and in a different way. This next scene is unlike the previous two. It is a detective scene where the team asks for a **country** and an **object**:

1. The detective is in a chartered airplane flying over the **country**. He is on a mission to find the **object**.
2. There is a villain on the plane who tries to trap the detective in his stateroom.
3. The detective uses the **object** to break down the door.
4. The villain escapes by parachuting out of the airplane.
5. The detective discovers the plane's pilot has been killed by the villain and he is forced to land the plane at the **country's** airport.

6. While he lands the plane, the villain's henchman steals the **object** from the plane.
7. The detective searches for clues and finds out the villain is at the factory.
8. The detective goes to the factory and gets captured by the villain, who ties him up and explains his master plan to populate the **country** with the **object** — starting with the one owned by the detective.
9. The detective is left to his own devices and he escapes. He tracks down the villain just in time before the villain activates his giant **object** which would help him rule the world.
10. The detective gives a monolog to the audience and mentions how he will never leave the **country** without the **object**.

Notice how it does not matter what the **object** or **country** is. The flags do not help the players use the suggestions in different ways. Consider all the elements that would remain static regardless of the suggestion: being on an airplane, trapping the detective in the stateroom, breaking down the door, parachuting, a dead pilot, etc. All the team does in a scene like this is follow a script and mention the **object** and **country** over and over again without ever using them. Recall the ability to use suggestion as explained in Chapter Eleven. Players must ensure that **all** flags facilitate the use of the suggestion rather than prevent its use.

Eventually the goal of a team should be to design structures that do not have flags. This is **extremely** difficult. It is not recommended for first-year teams. A non-flagged scene is one where the suggestion itself creates the structure. Only teams that are very comfortable with their improvisational skills and have had experience structuring with flags should attempt non-flagged structures. Non-flagged structures are really scenes where players "improvise" the structure as they go along!

Chapter Fifteen

Making Structures

Where do ideas come from?

Making a structure can be a hurdle for many beginning teams. The key is not to make them too complicated to begin with. Usually if teams practice the games described in the appendix over a period of time, structures will automatically surface. Many structures are just small variations on the games described there. For instance "The Hot Dog Stand" game (page 206) and the "Style Rollercoaster" game (page 223) could both be used as structures with only small changes.

Other structures could come from things in life. After seeing a murder mystery dinner, maybe an improviser wants to try to design a structure around it. Or a game could be based loosely on a television show or movie. (You could tell a *Titanic*-type plot line involving a different disaster.) If all players keep their eyes open, they should have no trouble coming up with ideas for structures.

Structures can also be designed around the talents of the team. If a team has a musician, consider designing a structure that takes advantage of that. If someone on the team can do magic, then maybe a structure could be designed that makes use of their sleight of hand (a silent movie perhaps?). It is a good idea to find out all of the other hobbies team members possess because they could come in handy.

Sometimes something will happen in practice that lends itself to being a structure. Maybe someone spontaneously begins narrating a story with a French accent. The scene works out well, so the team decides to create a structure set in revolutionary France. Just ensure that players are always conscious of the idea of structures during practices and a flash of creativity could be triggered.

How to decide which category a structure fits in

Sometimes a team creates a structure that does not fit neatly into one of the five categories. Other times, improvisers will sit down with the intent of designing a "who" structure or a "what" structure. Either way it is important that the structure does what it is supposed to do. By keeping focused on the goals of the events, it becomes a lot easier to make good structures.

A reminder that unless you are playing in the Canadian Improv Games or some other equally structured environment, it does not really matter if your structures neatly fit into a category. Explore and expand your options. Have fun.

Chapter Sixteen

"Who" Structures

Types of "who" structures

In general there are three archtypes when designing structures that focus on the "who." Most "who" structures fit somewhere within one of the three groups. When starting, you may wish to use these ideas as a base. Feel free to build beyond them. Some of the best structures will bear only a passing resemblance to these categories.

1. The one-characteristic who game

What the game is about

In this structure the team asks for one characteristic. (They usually ask for other things as well: objects, locations, etc.) The point of this game is to show that one characteristic in as many ways as possible. One player is usually designated as the major character, and this player will display the characteristic at all times and in as many ways as possible. The other players in the scene attempt to keep focus on that main character by "feeding" the characteristic (see Chapter Ten and "The Hot Dog Stand" game) as much as possible throughout the scene.

The other players still play "characters," but they choose their characteristics and attitudes so that they supplement the main character. The main character remains the focus throughout the scene.

What's good about it?

This game allows improvisers to explore one character fully and completely. Having only one characteristic to worry about permits lots of time to explore all the minor details about that character. If a team has one player who is very strong at characters it can allow them to shine. Additionally, if a team is very good at feeding, this game concept can allow for an excellent supporting cast.

What's bad about it?

Only having one character to explore can sometimes make it difficult to fill an entire four- to five-minute scene. Teams cannot afford to brush only the surface of the characteristic and must invent details about the character. A potential exists for the scene to grow unfocused as the players get distracted as they have only one source of material to draw from. Finally because only one player receives one characteristic, there is the possibility that the player, even an experienced one, may get an obscure or challenging characteristic that they have trouble presenting and the team has trouble feeding. In this disastrous scenario, there is no secondary or backup action to carry the scene.

Examples
- **Store owner:** The character works at a **location**. The boss, co-workers, wife, friends, and customers continually enter the store and feed the characteristic.
- **Life:** This game follows one character through time and shows how their characteristic operates at different stages of his/her life.

2. The two-character who game

What the game is about

This game centers on the interaction of two characters. They are usually placed in some sort of location or situation and are forced to deal with each other. The key in this game is to showcase how the two characteristics would interact. For example, *egotistical* would operate differently with *pessimistic* than it would with *angry*.

Other players will still be involved in feeding both players. Sometimes this game has a third main player who keeps the focus of the scene moving (sort of like a master of ceremonies).

What's good about it?

Seeing two characteristics interact can be very entertaining. Because teams receive two characteristics, they can decide which player has which (so the "hyper" player will not have to play a "sedated" character). Generally it is a good idea to have the person (referee, etc.) getting suggestions to select two characteristics which contrast with each other; this allows you more room for exploration and conflict. (Imagine the repetition in a scene with "happy" and "joyful.") Finally, because the players can choose which characteristic goes to which characters, they can create some interesting situations (like the bossy kid and cowardly teacher). This is the most commonly performed who-style game.

What's bad about it?

This version is probably the most neutral of the options (which is probably why it is done so often). A scene like this has the potential of having one player portray a far better character than the other, creating a very unbalanced scene. Background players have the responsibility of feeding and helping the character who needs more support in the exhibition of their characteristic. This style does not have as many distinct disadvantages as the others; instead, consider the advantages of the other options that this one does not have.

Examples

- **Desert Island:** Two characters are trapped on a desert island or other contained location and must escape with an **object**.
- **First day on the job:** The boss character has to deal with the new character on their first day at the **job**.

3. The three-/four-characteristic who game

What the game is about

This game puts a number of different characters in one place and watches the chaos which usually results. Sometimes these games evolve from two-characteristic games in which the team decides the master of ceremonies character gains a characteristic for himself. Non-character players in this game usually stay in the background as ample action is happening already with three or four characters.

What's good about it?

With the addition of a third character, more interaction becomes possible. Consider the possibility of having two-on-one situations and shifting alliances. Having a third characteristic also gives players the option of playing a funny but low-key character if it fits the suggestion (such as having the sleepy character say a few words at the beginning of the scene and then fall asleep downstage center and refuse to wake up for the duration of the scene). This would not be possible if teams are counting on that character to move the scene forward like they are in the one- or two-characteristic character games.

What's bad about it?

As soon as teams break the two-character barrier, it becomes increasingly difficult to show all of the characters. Some characters may shine, but others may be left in the background. Teams have to ensure that they are presenting *all* the suggestions, which means playing all of the characters to the fullest — a challenging feat. Each character should get a turn in the limelight. This is especially true for the four-characteristic game. When teams have that many people, it becomes almost essential to have a master of ceremonies or moderator who controls the action.

Examples

- **Waiting room:** A number of characters are waiting for **something**.
- **Talk show:** The host of the talk show keeps the characters on track while they talk about the **topic**.

Derivatives of the who games

Character groups

In these versions, each characteristic is given to a group of characters. Either all the characteristics are given to groups or some to groups and some to individuals.

- **One group:** The commander of a military unit deals with his characteristic unit.
- **Two groups:** Two rival gangs have to team up to battle the police.
- **Three groups:** The players, coaches, and announcers of the **sport** all have different characteristics.

Changing characteristics

In this version, either the characteristics or players change during the scene.

- **Changing life:** Tells the story of a character's life and how an **event** changed his/her outlook on life.
- **Characteristic tag:** A characteristic travels through the team whenever the character touches someone else.
- **Changing players:** Different players, who take turns on- and off-stage, take the role of the same character.
- **Two-one characteristics:** Two shorter scenes each explore a single characteristic. Usually some sort of link exists between the two.
- **Changing group:** Everyone in the scene changes from one characteristic to the next through the scene.

Alternative ask-fors

Some teams take a basic structure from their game and make it different by asking for a source of an improvised character from something other than a characteristic. They take these things and base their characters on them. Some possible ask-fors include famous people, memories, stereotypes, magazines, animals, physical objects, and occupations. Finally, do not be afraid to experiment with even more exotic structures that do not fit in these simple categories — originality is always appreciated.

Chapter Seventeen

"What" Structures

Types of "what" structures

The "what" question is the most open of the categories. Stressing the "what" basically means telling a story, which is something that most scenes will do automatically. Storytelling is something that is built into our society. Teams quickly discover that most of their "who" and "how" events will tell stories as well. If a game does not tell a story, it is often unsatisfying. (Although remember that this is the only category where a story is really required!)

When designing structures focusing on the "what," teams must be sure to stress the story element. The audience should not have to search to find the beginning, middle, and end, no more so than they should search to find the characters in a "who" game. The plot should progress naturally and logically. Teams should keep these ideas in mind when designing structures.

In general there are three typical ways to design a "what" structure. Either the team tells a new, never-before-heard story, they tell a pre-planned story with significant changes, or they ask for a well-know story and tell it in a different way. It takes much less skill to simply retell an old story without the twist. Teams that tell famous tales are basically reciting something they have heard and potentially practiced before. The audience wants to see improv, so teams should treat them to something new or something old in a new way.

The format teams use to tell stories can vary too. Some teams choose to have a single narrator (as in the "Typewriter" game). Other teams choose to tell a story as a pair with two narrators working together — or against each other. Stories can be told or shown as a group without any narrator at all. Whatever method teams choose will alter the focus of the scene.

Because stories can be presented so many different ways and

the definition of good storytelling and good stories is so subjective, any division of the "what" category is very difficult. What follows is our best attempt to deal with the concept in sections. Remember that there is much overlap (telling a new story in a weird way) and that teams should not limit themselves to categories but should seek to invent their own style of storytelling.

1. New stories

In this type of story the team tells a story which has never been told before. This is really the most open of the improv structure types. Anything is possible as long as the scene has a sequence of related events with a clearly identifiable starting point, conflict, rising action, climax, and conclusion. A limitless number of options exists for teams interested in creating a new story.

- **The title:** The team asks for a title (of a non-existent work) for the story they are going to tell. The team presents the story in the format they have chosen while basing all of the action on the title they were given.
- **Mixed-up elements:** The team asks for unrelated elements that comprise the core of their story. For example, they may ask for an injury and a location and tell the story of how someone obtained that injury at that location.
- **Linked elements:** The team asks for one thing and something else related to the first suggestion. The team then illustrates the connection between the things. For example, they may ask for an occupation and something that could go wrong for that occupation.
- **Origin story:** Asking for something and telling either its entire history or a portion of it (its beginning or what will happen to it in the future). This can also be done for people (i.e., why was Einstein so smart?).

2. Bring the story along

For this structure the team bases their scene's plot around a well-known story from literature, television, or movies. Teams take that basic plot and change it by using the suggestion (for example, setting it in a new location). Teams using this approach must ensure that the structure changes significantly every time. (The plot should focus on the improvised elements and not be filled with stock lines and actions.) Teams can present a wide variety of stories using this format.

- *Charlie and the Chocolate Factory*: A child's adventures in the factory of their *favorite thing.*
- *Titanic*: The story of two lovers set against the backdrop of a *disaster.*
- *Lord of the Flies*: Telling the same story of the kids trapped in a different *location.*

3. Ask for the story

In this format the team asks for a well-known story which they retell in an unusual way. Usually the team asks for a fairy tale, although alternatives exist (a Bible story or a nursery rhyme, for example). Teams tell the story in a different format, or (more commonly) ask for things that will change the story.

- **Weak genre:** A story told in a way that is not a genre but is a unique way of telling a story (for example, a fairy tale presented from the perspective of German nihilists).
- **Different point of view:** A story told from the point of view of one of the minor characters. (The play *Rosencrantz and Guildenstern Are Dead*, which tells the tale of *Hamlet* from the viewpoint of a pair of courtiers, is an example of this concept.)
- **Weird link:** The story is told with the addition of some other factor (for example, an occupation of the main character). This idea also includes putting in characters that would not normally belong, such as *Dracula* in the *Three Little Pigs*, or Winston Churchill in *Little Red Riding Hood.*

Ways of telling stories

When a team decides to tell a story, they can choose to do so in a couple of different ways. Each method has advantages and disadvantages. Any one of the different types of stories described above could be told in any one of these ways. Mixing and matching to achieve different outcomes is a key facet of improv.

Method #1 — With a narrator

What this game is about

When improv first started, almost every team would perform what-style games with a narrator. The narrator (usually one of the team's strongest players) tells a story while the rest of the team acts it out (very similar to the "Typewriter" game). A story told by a narrator can be controlled in one of two ways. The narrator can dictate actions that the players will perform, either in mime or with a line or two of supporting dialog. Story advancement could also take place by the players, whose actions would be commented upon by the narrator. Ideally, a mix of narrator and team control would exist, creating a balanced collaboration of a story.

What's good about it?

With one narrator telling the story, it is easier to keep the story on track. One person takes responsibility to make sure the story has a plot with a beginning, middle, and end. Stories set up this way look the most like "stories" and the audience will clearly understand what is going on. If a team has a player who is very strong, that individual can be made the storyteller and can be allowed to shine. Finally, having a narrator means the story can have "bridges" from one part to the next much more cleanly than if they were forced to rely on team consensus. These bridge times (if not used too much) can give the team time to figure out what is going to happen next.

What's bad about it?

A team can start to rely on their narrator too much. It is easy to let the person telling the story do all the work. Ideally the team and the narrator will work together to tell the story with one giving ideas to the other. This does not always happen in practice, so pay attention for it. If the entire team is not contributing to the scene, it means that there are less people coming up with ideas. In general, a group of heads is better than one.

Method #2 — With two narrators

What this game is about

An expansion on the narrator method is adding a second narrator. These two players tell the story in tandem. Other than that, the structure is very similar to the one-narrator option. Often, the two narrators assume a character, contrasting with the usually neutral status of a solo narrator. Children discussing a situation, police officers making a report, or two criminals explaining what went wrong to their boss are examples of this characterization of the narrators. The narrators could be opposites or enemies (the devil and God, good conscience and bad conscience, etc.). Oftentimes this structure will have a third player who acts as the person to whom the storytellers are telling the story. This main character acts as a filter to make sure the story is still coherent and the narrators are not contradicting each other.

What's good about it?

With two players working together to tell the story, teams have twice as many ideas in the storyteller section. If the two players exhibit good chemistry together, this option can be quite entertaining. This method also spreads the burden of the storytelling. One can start things off and then the other can pick things up. If a team lacks one very strong player, this method can make up for that by using two good players.

What's bad about it?

Having two players means there must be some compromise. The players must learn to work together to tell the story. They have to pay attention to what each is saying and be sure not to contradict one another. The other danger is that many teams using this structure use their two best players to tell the story. This means that the story is enacted by less skilled improvisers. This puts more burden on the storytellers. As well, the pair of narrators may spend too much time bantering and not enough time focusing on the plot elements of the story. *(This game is about story, not about witty dialog.)*

85

Method #3 — With no narrators

What this game is about

Some teams choose to tell a story without any narrators at all. The entire team acts together to tell a story. At first the idea of a narrator-less story seems unusual, but upon consideration of most films and plays, how many of them have narrators? A small modification of this method is to have the narrator in the story. In that case the narrator will interact in the scene for parts of the action and then turn and talk to the audience to explain what is going on. Both methods have advantages and disadvantages.

What's good about it?

This method allows the entire team to work together directly to tell the story. All of the skills players learned in the "Improv Foundations" chapter come together in creating the improvised story. The group can also show off its ability to work as a team in a fairly obvious way. If teams choose the option of putting the narrator into the story, it allows for the advantages of both methods.

What's bad about it?

Working together like this without any structure can be dangerous. Pacing a story properly can be difficult when everyone is involved. For this method to work, the group must really work as a team. Often when things do not work out perfectly, one or two players will take control of scenes and it will turn into a narrated scene without a narrator — basically two players telling the whole story *and* acting it out. This combination by a pair does not allow a team to show the depth of their talent and limits the number of ideas that can be contributed to the story.

Chapter Eighteen

"How" Structures

The "how" is the way in which a scene is presented. It can be thought of as the "style" of the presentation or the genre in which it is presented. Talk shows, horrors, and children's pop-up books are some examples of the immense number of different genres that exist in theatre, literature, or film. Any "how" event should demonstrate the team's ability to display the specific elements of a genre and, more importantly, how these affect the suggestions.

Types of "how" structures

Portraying the "how" is the most difficult of the concepts to perform well — it is also one of the most entertaining to watch when it is done well. When teams are designing their structure, it is critical that they create a structure that allows improvisational exploration of the elements of the chosen genre. Squeezing all of the genre's elements into a scene without over-structuring the presentation is often challenging. Many teams will use their structure's flags to "plug in" elements from the style instead of improvising them. Go back and reread Chapter Fourteen ("Flags") — **flags exist to help the improv and not to stop it.** Any elements from the style should be presented in such a way that the suggestion plays a key role — teams should remember that when designing "how" games.

Creating a "how" structure can be seen as a series of choices. Generally, the first choice is selecting a genre. After a genre is decided upon, the other choices can be made at a leisurely pace.

Choice #1: How to choose a genre

Picking a genre that the team admires or has a background in simplifies the team's work. If a team attempted to present a musical when no one on the team has ever seen one, it will likely miss including many of its elements. Try playing "Style Rollercoaster" and its variations to try out a lot of styles in a short amount of time. If a genre works well, go back over it and spend some more time on it.

After you have an idea of the genre you would like to do (also take a look at the [incomplete] list in the appendix), do some research on it. Make sure you know all of its elements. If the genre is literary, read some example books. If it is media based, watch movies or television shows related to it. If your genre is rare (for example, Japanese Noh theatre) try checking out libraries which often have videotapes you can borrow to watch. If for some reason you cannot research a genre, it is often best not to do it at all.

When you have seen a number of examples of the genre make a list of the elements that these sources have in common. When you design your flags, make sure they use these elements. When you decide what you are asking the audience for, make sure it will change every single one of the elements in some significant way. Remember that characters are not elements. You could do the style of James Bond, but it would not include James Bond. (For example, the *Three Little Pigs* could start with them bungy jumping out of their old houses. They could be high rollers with lots of pig-women at their sides. The wolf would be an evil mastermind, etc.) Try talking through some fairy tales and things that would change under your choice of genre.

Choice #2: Parody or genuine?

There are two very different ways to present every genre. They could be presented as a genuine example by including the stylistic elements that define the style or they could be presented as a parody, using spoofs and gags to mock elements of the style. For example, The Austin Powers movies were parodies of the James Bond genre, while *The Saint* was a genuine example of the same style. The end results are very different.

If a group is trying for maximum humor, then a parody is a stronger comic choice. Many styles, when taken out of context and placed on an improv stage, are very simple to parody. Note that a style is defined by a set of elements, and parody is only an effective tool when many of these elements are mocked and presented.

The second option is to play the style straight. If the style is a humorous style to begin with, parody becomes unnecessary. If your genre is comic farce or Dr. Seuss, the style itself contains enough humor to take you through a scene. Even if the genre is not a funny one, you are not required to play it as a parody. Improv does not have to be funny. Some of the best (and in competition, the highest scoring) scenes were not funny at all. As long as your scene is entertaining, enjoyable to watch, and uses the elements of the style, you have done a good job. Styles in the past that have been done "straight" include Native American legends, theatre of the absurd, Japanese Kabuki theatre, and Shakespearean historical plays. Do not feel constricted by a narrow definition of improv. Try and expand the horizons. Improv would not be what it is today if every team did the same old things.

Choice #3: Do you keep it in the genre?

Say you have decided to do your genre as a 1950s sitcom. You decide to play it as a satire of the types of shows that existed back then. Your next choice is whether or not to have the scene take place in the 1950s. You could play the entire scene as something that could have been seen on TV in the '50s. In this case your ask-for could be a family problem or a misunderstanding. That would allow you to play a scene very similar to the original type of show. This is not your only option.

You could ask for something that will take that genre somewhere else. Imagine asking for a location. Now instead of taking place in a house in the '50s, it could be happening in a jungle. Even in this weird location you would be expected to show all of the elements of the style. The cheesy characters, the nosy neighbor, the wholesome family, and the daily moral would all have to exist in this unusual setting.

Every genre you choose will have a similar choice. Do you show the style as it was originally portrayed, or do you move it to a new setting or situation? Shakespeare could be told with the use of kings and princes, or it could just as easily take place in a

89

modern family home. Just make sure you keep the elements. Both choices are fine and can be equally entertaining. You may even want to try out both options to see which one you like better. Explore and see what works for your particular scene in your particular genre.

Choice #4: Do you tell a story?

You may tell a story with your presentation, but it is not required that you do so. Many genres tell a story as part of their essential elements, but an equally large number do not. For the genres that do not automatically tell a story, you will have to decide if you want to tell one or not. Consider this short list of genres that do not normally tell stories:

- Infomercial
- Bloopers show
- Magazine styles (i.e., *Teen* magazine, *Muscle and Fitness*, *Rolling Stone*)
- Televised entertainment news magazine
- News broadcast
- Science show
- Talk show

There are many more. Even these styles could be set up as a story, but it is not required that they are. (Imagine telling *Little Red Riding Hood* as an infomercial. They could be trying to sell just about everything in the story, or maybe it could be something that *Little Red Riding Hood* was missing that if she had, she could have taken down the wolf.)

Push the boundaries of the "how" game. Just be familiar with what the boundaries are.

Chapter Nineteen

"Use of Suggestion" Structures

Types of "use of suggestion" structures

This chapter describes methods of planning structures for scenes based on one simple suggestion. The same structuring principles hold for concepts (peace, opposites, life), objects (table, cloud, computer), people (janitor, Ronald Reagan, teenager), or any other concise thought. The idea of this category of game is to explore a simple suggestion in a creative manner.

Although teams are encouraged to discover other ways of presenting use-of-suggestion structures, it is recommended that teams develop their ability to perform the vignette before attempting to create structures that are significantly different from it.

1. The vignette game

How the suggestion is explored

The suggestion is explored by examining many of its different aspects in various situations or settings.

What the game is about

The team presents the suggestion in a number of different settings and situations by performing a series of vignettes. These vignettes are set up like very short stories (see Chapter Eight). The team starts a routine and then breaks it, usually in a humorous way. Abandoning the completed story, the team moves on to a new vignette. Either the routine or how it is broken must relate to the suggestion in some way. The hope is that the breaking of the routine will be the punch line of the scene.

Different variations of the game have vignettes of different lengths. Usually one can expect each individual scene to be between ten seconds and a minute.

What's good about it?

The vignette game has become the method of choice for the exploration of the suggestions and for good reason. Its format allows a team to examine a large number of different aspects to a suggestion in a very short time. If the team has a lot of ideas about the suggestion, they can present them all very quickly. If the depth of talent on the team is high (i.e., the weakest player on the team is still very strong), it allows every member of the team to have their moment in the spotlight.

Due to the fact that the vignette structure moves so fast, it is an excellent training method for all of the other games a team will explore. The vignette is an excellent opportunity to show off the team's basic improv skills which are not as obvious in the more structured events.

What's bad about it?

Performing the use-of-suggestion format as a vignette requires that the team possess an adequate level of improv ability. In order for the scene to work there can be no blocking, wimping or delaying (see Chapter Three). The team must really work together to make sure the scenes work. Players should be comfortable starting a scene knowing that their teammates will be able to finish it in a flourish. The entire team must be ready to jump in and "break" the established routines. Breaking a routine can be particularly difficult when the routine itself does not match the suggestions. In that case, the breaking of the routine must involve both the routine and the suggestion. This game requires a lot of fast thinking and reflexes.

In addition, because there is usually no connection from one scene to the next, everyone on the team must be thinking of ideas for the future. Creating new ideas is challenging for players who are involved in the scene that is taking place. A high-quality team can count on the players who are not directly involved with the main action in a vignette to come up with the starting point for the next scene — on a team with a more shallow talent pool, trouble emerges when all the skilled players are involved with a scene that the background players cannot end.

The vignette game can be operated so that it is a direct duplicate of the freeze game. A line of players wait to "clap-in" to each scene. Every vignette has two actors and a bunch of players standing in the back watching. (In the worst case, these background players are talking to each other, planning the next scenes.) These versions of the vignette game are not nearly as fun to watch — the audience is distracted by the background conversations. More importantly, scenes with a pair of people speaking fail to show the "wheres" of their vignettes. (The frantic pace of the vignette makes it easy for players to forget to create the five Ws.) A more impressive and more entertaining vignette would be one in which all the players in a scene are physicalizing the action. (Look at the physicalizing games in the appendix for hints on learning how to do this.)

A final problem that often occurs in the vignette game is the failure to explore the suggestion adequately. Recall that the advantage to this use-of-suggestion format is the ability to explore a large number of different aspects in a short period of time. **Quantity does not equal quality.** A high number of vignettes presented that really only touch the surface of **one** aspect of the suggestion **is not exploration** — it is a failure of a vignette scene. The number of scenes presented by a team does not matter if the scenes do not explore a wide range of different things or a smaller number of things in a deep manner.

The vignette game, by its very nature, makes it difficult to delve deeply into any one aspect of the suggestion (which is a method of exploration). It is generally limited to exploring a wide variety of aspects. Teams interested in exploring the suggestion in a detailed manner should look to a structure other than the vignette.

Examples of vignette derivatives

- **Straight Vignette:** After each routine is broken, a player from the background steps up to the front and starts a new scene. The rest of the players accept offers and either become characters in the new vignette or objects in the environment.
- **Freeze Game:** New scenes start when one of the players

"claps in." All of the actors in the scene freeze and the new player takes the position of one of the old players. A new vignette starts and everyone else changes to become objects in the new location.

- **Call the Players:** New scenes start by a player calling out which players they want to be main characters in the next vignette. Everyone else becomes objects/background.
- **Call the Location:** This format explores a variety of wheres by having new scenes start by a player yelling out a new location that the other players then form to begin a new scene, set in and connecting the suggestion to the location.
- **Call the Style:** This format explores a variety of hows by having new scenes start by a player yelling out a new style in which the team will explore the suggestion.
- **Chain Vignette:** The first scene has one main player (the rest are objects), the second scene has two players, the third three players, etc., until all of the players are in the eighth scene. The vignettes then go backwards and revisit all of the earlier scenes until there is only one player again.
- **Links:** Each vignette links to the next somehow (maybe by an object, maybe a character, maybe a word).

Important note and hint for the vignette game

There is one important trick that some teams have discovered for the vignette game. Instead of coming up with the vignettes on-stage during the scene, they plan out (either consciously or unconsciously) a series of "set locations" or "set scenarios" that they can play out and "link" to the theme. For example, the team may perform a vignette based on *Dragonheart* (the movie about the last dragon in the world). It could be linked to just about any theme:

- **Theme: Patience**

    "But Draco, you just have to wait. Sooner or later people will stop killing your kind. Someday people and dragons can live in peace."

    "But there are no more. I am the last one!"

- **Theme: Industry**

    "We must get these factories built. We cannot do it alone.

We need the strength of a thousand dragons if we are to succeed."
"But there are no more. I am the last one!"
• **Theme: Patterns**
"First we killed the mammoths. Then we killed the Great Auks. Then we killed the passenger pigeon. How long 'til all the dragons are gone?"
"It's too late. There are no more. I am the last one!"

This process can be done for every theme. Teams can develop a whole series of these set scenarios or locations and then just plug them into the theme they are given. Some teams do not intentionally pre-plan these situations — it just happens. A great moment during practice inspires a player to resurrect it during a performance. Other teams use this regurgitation of witty ideas and clever locations as part of their strategy and choreograph a whole series of funny situations or eye-pleasing locations which they then proceed to link to whatever suggestion the team presents.

There is nothing wrong with stock characters

This use of stock characters, situations, and settings is not "cheating." The main danger from relying on this method is the difficulty in linking some suggestions to the set scenes, which end up looking forced, awkward, or confusing. The breakdown of the scene shows that the team's structure has overshadowed their ability to improvise.

Spontaneously creating clever situations with inventive physical actions makes improv teams look brilliantly skilled and psychically linked to novice audiences. Experienced audiences and anyone with improv know-how is well aware of the team's pre-established pattern. Prearranging characters, locations, and situations is an accepted method of setting up a vignette game, but when a vignette is performed this way, teams must be careful about the way that the routine (which will relate to the preset plan and not the suggestion) is broken. The routine must be broken by something strongly linked to the suggestion. If not, the scene is overstructured and the team's overplanned script is embarrassingly revealed to a tired audience.

The best way to perform a use-of-suggestion vignette game is to aim to avoid set locations/scenarios and to search out ways in which to explore the theme during the huddle and while in the background of a scene. This style of scene is of higher quality and is more impressive but a lot more difficult. Teams will have to evaluate the level of their players and select the most appropriate format for the game. A key to not using set locations/scenarios — teams still have to **prove** that the scenes are improvised and not preplanned. If a team is challenging itself to create vignettes on the fly but the scenes still appear as though they were pre-set, then nothing has been accomplished by refusing to use set plans.

2. The set location/scenario game

How this game explores the suggestion

The suggestion is explored either by examining many of its different aspects in one setting or by exploring a smaller number of aspects in more detail.

What the game is about

The team decides on one setting or scenario for the scene and then explores the suggestion within those boundaries. (Advanced teams will choose that setting based on their suggestion.) Scenes based on locations have a variety of characters coming and passing through the scene and "feeding" the suggestion every time they enter. Similarly, a scene with an individual enduring an ordeal or living an average day will have events related to the suggestion happen to them. The other players use the same technique of "feeding" the suggestion by entering and interacting with the main character.

What's good about it?

This game immediately comes across as being different from the far more common vignette game. Anything different has a distinct advantage.

This game allows teams that have a few stand-out players to put those players in major roles. In the vignette game, everyone must contribute almost equally. The team can put more focus on the players they choose. There is far more structure with the set location/scenario format and teams can figure out where the scene is going a lot more effectively than the "vignette."

Should the team choose to explore less aspects of the theme and focus on a smaller number in greater detail, this format allows for that better than the vignette. If the team wished to contrast two of the aspects that they find most important, they will find this format very compatible with their plan.

What's bad about it?

The choice of the setting for this structure can limit the amount of exploration in the scene. For example, if the suggestion is "fame" and they have set your scene in a kitchen, showing famous landmarks or famous historical events may prove difficult. This structure is intrinsically much more limiting than the open-ended vignette.

By the very act of structuring, the use-of-suggestion event teams have increased the danger that their scenes will become "over-structured." Teams must remain cautious that the structure does not overshadow their ability to improvise.

Examples

- **Blank family:** The family is the exaggerated model of the suggestion and everything they do or say relates to the suggestion in some way.
- **Day in the life:** The main character gets up in the morning and moves through a day interacting with various people and having the suggestion come out in everything that happens.
- **Television show:** The team takes on the roles of the characters from a television show and shows the suggestion through the activities in the show.
- **Shop/restaurant/park/school:** The entire scene takes place in a standard location where people come through showing the suggestion in different ways.

Chapter Twenty

Reality-Based Structures

How is this kind of structure unique?

Most people relate improvisation directly with humor. Most of this book has been spent developing the skills needed to create humorous scenes. A little of the "how" event touched on the idea that scenes can be entertaining without having to be funny. This whole chapter is based on that concept.

This chapter describes the structuring and planning of scenes that are based on real depictions of human life, explored in a more sincere manner than the standard improv antics. Players who excel at comedic performance may experience trouble with this emphasis on sincerity — the best players are as comfortable presenting genuine emotion as they are delivering punch lines. A reality-based improv scene can be presented in a multitude of ways, but the common element in any of them is the showcasing of true feelings. This kind of improv can be thought of as an "acting" category, but that would be a misnomer — spontaneously creating a scene capable of exploring depth of sincerity is a better description.

To structure or not to structure?

Structuring this type of game is optional. An easy option is to ask the audience for a scenario and then reenact the scene with an emphasis on emotion and feeling. In general, attempts at structuring harm the resulting scenes more than they help, since the preplanned elements encroach on the genuine feel of the scene. Abandoning structure is not the solution, as using a very flexible structure can enhance and focus the scene's action. Structuring is also necessary if a team chooses to undertake the risk of creating an entirely new concept for a sincere scene (such as a scene in mime or Shakespearean prose).

Before a team considers structuring this event, they should be comfortable playing it as a traditional form without any structure at all. Only then will they be confident that the structure they are adding will help the event rather than hurt it.

Working on the basic skills specialized for this event should precede structuring practices.

The huddle — the who, what and where

Success in a reality-based improv game starts with the huddle. If the team does not have a good huddle and does not interpret the suggestion correctly, the scene will fail. Reality-based improv could also be called "listening" improv. The team must listen carefully to their given suggestion and remember it for the duration of the scene — the suggestion is the source of all the action throughout the scene. No matter how skilled a team is, if they forget, blur, or sidestep the suggestion they will not do well in a game of this type.

So the team has listened carefully to the scenario, now what? In the huddle the team must consider the Ws. If the team chooses to ask for a scenario, first break it down into its parts and think about the **whens**. If there are two parts to the scenario, make sure that the entire team understands each part. For example:

The team is presenting a scene based on the idea, "You have done something wrong. Now you try to make amends."

This suggestion should be broken down to:

1. You did something wrong (in the past).
2. You are trying to make amends (in the present).

Another example: "Your best does not seem to be good enough."

1. You have done your best (in the past).
2. It wasn't good enough (in the past).

The team should try doing this exercise with a large number of scenarios. (This exercise will work with sincere or silly scenarios.)

After the "when" has been understood, the team should move onto the **what**. Scenarios and audience suggestions are usually quite general — a phrase or two. The responsibility of creating the specific details falls onto the team. Review the example again.

"You have done something wrong. Now you try to make amends."

The team should decide immediately **what** was done wrong and **what** the character is doing to make amends. Think of the possibilities:

- They cheated on a test. They are going to admit it to the teacher.
- They told a secret they said they would not. They are trying to apologize.
- They missed their friend's graduation. They attempt to take them out for dinner.

Have the team sit in a circle and discuss many possibilities. Make sure that the idea for the "what" is defined early and is well understood.

After having decided upon the "what," the **who** should become fairly apparent. In most cases, the team should try to have a who that bears resemblance to themselves (the same age, interests, etc.). Playing a character of dramatically different backgrounds, beliefs, and ideals looks forced, awkward, and at times, unbelievable. Consider possible who's for the earlier choices:

- The person who cheated and their friend who also cheated.
- The person who told the secret and the person to whom they are apologizing.
- The friend who graduated and the person who missed it.

As part of the "who," the team should decide which player will play each character and the relationship between the characters (i.e., longtime friends, acquaintances, boy/girlfriend, brothers, etc.). How many whos are involved and how they interact may be improvised on the spot or part of a preplanned structure (see next page).

The final W to be decided upon is the **where**. Sometimes the where will come about from the scenario given (It's the last day of school and ...) or from the team's created what (She is leaving on a bus and ...). Other times any where can be chosen. Make sure that the team decides on a location that the scene will be set in. There is nothing worse than an issue/event taking place on a blank stage.

The first ten seconds — defining the action

When the scene starts, it is easy to start wimping and waffling (see Chapter Three). Perhaps the huddle was chaotic with little being resolved or with team members leaving with different understandings. Sometimes everyone knows where the scene is going but everyone is afraid to take it there. Scenes that begin poorly, with no action or progression whatsoever, are often difficult to turn around.

"So, how's it going?"

"All right, I guess ... "

"Did you see that movie last night?"

"No, I stayed home."

Ugh! Scenes should not start out this way! These scenes should start at the important part of the conversation. Define what is happening early so that it can be explored. Wimping and waffling must be prevented — especially in the crucial beginning stages.

The core of the scene — genuine exploration of the issue

When the scene starts moving, it is important to remember to keep the tone genuine. Avoid launching into melodramatic monologs. Avoid breaking down and crying when there is a minute left to "show your range." Avoid entering and adding to the scene some "comic relief." Avoid being extremely upset about something that a normal person would not be that upset about. Avoid gagging or playing "characters."

This type of event can be the most challenging to perform. They are certainly the hardest to make entertaining. You cannot "yuk it up" with the audience in this category. Walking the fine line between over-drama and over-comedy can be very difficult. Do not wimp out when you are on-stage and fall back to making the audience laugh. Do not wimp out of showing genuine feeling with playing "dramatic" characters. Players benefit from playing themselves or someone like themselves — a more natural scene will develop.

Then what? Raising the stakes

In a few minutes it can be hard to explore an entire emotional event. The trick is to intensify the situation, compressing the action

101

in a passably realistic manner. Identical to a scene telling a story, extra action needs a raising of the stakes. Adding a plethora of emotionally destructive elements is not effective raising of the stakes. Consider this example:

"Why can't you just tell me why you are breaking up with me!"

"I'm pregnant."

"Oh no ... "

"And my father is beating me!"

"Then let me help you."

"Just like you helped me through my anorexia?!"

"I told you I'm sorry, it's just ... "

"It doesn't matter; I'm getting an abortion."

"No, I can help — just let me get off the crack."

"Crack?! I thought you got off that stuff on that night you tried to shoot yourself?!"

"Stop! The inner demons are tearing me apart!"

Eek! Raising the stakes does not have to involve catastrophic events. Raising the stakes takes what is already happening and makes it more important, puts a time deadline on it, or involves more people. Let's look at one of the previous examples and explore "good ways" to raise the stakes:

Scenario: "You have done something wrong. Now you try to make amends."

What: They cheated on a test. They are going to admit it to the teacher.

Who: The person who cheated and their friend who also cheated.

Raise the stakes:

• The friend needs the marks to get into college.

• If the friend gets caught, he will get thrown out of school.

• Someone else will take the blame if the person does not admit things.

• He owes the friend a favor, and he asks him not to tell.

• He was the one who got his friend to cheat in the first place.

• His younger brother finds out and is disappointed.

Throughout the scene the team should be thinking of ways to

make things harder. They do not have to bring in crazy problems, they just have to think about things that would make the problem more important and take on a greater significance. The players in the scene should always be thinking of ways to make things more difficult for themselves. (It's easy to wimp out and make things easy in these scenes.) The players in the back should always be thinking of ways to enter the scene and feed more tension by **raising the stakes**.

The end — resolution?

The scene will eventually have to end. Just like in real life everything does not have to be resolved after a few minutes. The team should do its best to have some sort of ending, but whether or not anything was solved is unimportant. A reality-based improv scene is not a story game. There does not have to be a beginning, middle, and end. As long as the team does things genuinely, success has been achieved. Explore the suggestion. Be real. The scene will help create itself.

Structuring reality-based events

Now that the team is comfortable performing the event without a structure, they may wish to explore some of their options. Be warned — structuring this category may decrease the level of quality as it hampers spontaneity of emotion. This section is included to give teams the option to structure these games. One noteworthy idea: Structuring can emerge unconsciously as teams continually gravitate toward certain issues, emotions, relationships, or general plots. Teams should evaluate their reality-based games and consider whether or not structure exists — being aware of the advantages and disadvantages of structuring should be considered either way.

Structuring can also help this event. Some of the best and most interesting performances come about because of creative structuring. Being frightened of using structures will prevent teams from exploring the use of creative structures. Exploring all the possibilities is the easiest way to guarantee success for a team.

Structuring the "who"

There are two possible elements of structuring that can happen involving the "who."

The players

This is the first structuring step most teams will take. The team decides either consciously or unconsciously that one or two players are stronger at the event. The team then decides that those two players will be in the game no matter what. This can work out well when those two players have a chemistry that they develop over the year that shows up on-stage. It can be bad when the scenes they are in grow stale and turn out the same every time. The other danger with setting players is that other people grow lax. The background players may stop learning how to play the game. When it would be advantageous for them to play a role in a scenario (for example, if the scenario progresses to the point where one of the main players walks out of the scene at two minutes), they do not have the skills to do so (or they are hesitant about entering a scene when they should).

Choosing main players is a method of specialization that can help when it works but cuts down a team's options when it does not.

The characters

Taking it a step further, some teams will structure the relationship between the characters into the scene. Sometimes this is done consciously, but more commonly it happens when a team falls into a rut of doing the same sort of scene over and over again. No matter what the suggestion is, the team plays the boyfriend-girlfriend relationship or the father-son relationship (remember the warning about playing people much older than the players) or the brother-brother relationship. Keeping options open is helpful. Any limitations teams place on themselves make it harder to play the suggestion.

A better method to structure the who is to come up with a "format" around which the scene is structured. The format that has been used most often in the past is to have two players talk to each

104

other while others enter during the scene and raise the stakes. Many teams use this structure without realizing that it is a structure. Here are other ways a scene can be explored:

- First minute — player A and player B; second minute — player A and player C; last two minutes — important scene with player B and player C.
- Group scene with everyone interacting with everyone. The team must be very good at sharing focus for this to work.
- Three main players interacting while the others act as "feeders."

Think about exploring beyond the two-players-talking structure.

Structuring the "where"

This is a more legitimate area to structure. Since the issue game must be done in a real and genuine manner, most teams choose to have the scene performed in something nice and simple. Most teams will choose a location that can allow for some privacy for the main characters but still allow the other players to enter and "feed" the scene. Since most scenarios are open-ended enough that they could take place anywhere, teams can decide what location they will be using during their rehearsals. For teams that do not wish to go that far, there is the option of "designing" a library of locations that the team can choose from when they perform their scene. Ninety percent of these types of scenes take place in either libraries (or classrooms), school hallways, living rooms (or bedrooms), or restaurants (or coffeehouses). If the team has already practiced making these locations, it is one less thing to think about in the (rather full) huddle.

Be wary of getting too caught up with these prefabricated locations. Sometimes an excellent opportunity will come up to set a scene somewhere the team might not have thought of in practice. If a team is too caught up in their set locations they may miss a wonderful chance. Consider the suggestion "this is the end of something important" — a team that sets their scene in an airport terminal with the ending of a relationship is using spontaneity

105

to create a more suitable scene than the team that set their scene in a cafe.

Structuring an exotic location

Sometimes the team may come up with something very unusual in practice that they may wish to use as their "set" issue location. They then twist their issue so that it fits the location. There are varying degrees of uniqueness. Teams may set their events in:

- a pool hall
- a car
- on a boat
- an improv practice

If the team has an unusual idea, they may wish to think about creating a structure. "Twisting" the scenario too far may dilute the genuine sincerity of the scene. Always prioritize the suggestion above any structure developed. Teams should be prepared to drop a "set location" if it does not fit the suggestion.

Structuring the "what"

This is the most dangerous element to structure in a reality-based event. Some teams in the past go into competitions with the notion that they are going to "twist" their suggestion to fit their pre-decided issue. It is common for these teams to have a short list (either consciously or unconsciously) of issues they are comfortable playing and then just picking one to fit the suggestion. Common choices include: anorexia, abuse, racism, abortion, and homophobia. These teams believe that presenting "big" issues will impress the audience.

Tragedies of amazing severity are not what reality-based events are about. Sincere improv is about playing *any* situation in a real, genuine way. Teams are certainly not helping themselves by preplanning what conflict they will use — nine times out of ten, teams will twist the scenario too far and end up "playing" the tragedy instead of following the suggestion.

It is recommended that you avoid playing any issue you already did in practice. What generally happens is the team falls back into playing the same scene they did before. In doing so they often completely miss the suggestion they were given. Better to improvise a new scene than try to recreate something you did before.

Structuring the "how"

Almost all of these events will be done with a "normal" how. The team will play a scene using genuine emotion and realistic settings. This is the easiest way to perform a reality-based event (seeing as that is what reality is like), and yet it is still very hard to do it well. Sometimes a team may wish to take a risk and do things slightly (or very) differently. Some small changes in the how that may be presented:

- **Internal thoughts:** Other players verbalize the thoughts of the main characters.
- **Soliloquies:** At a moment of tension, the main player launches into a monolog.
- **Dream sequence:** The main player fantasizes about what "could have" happened.
- **Voices:** The main characters hear voices from people they look up to.
- **Flashbacks:** The scene flashes back to some earlier point to get a better understanding of the character(s).

The ask-for

Asking for a scenario is not the only option in a reality-based scene. The team may wish to ask for more creative things. These are just some possibilities to get a scene started:

- An important moment in someone's life
- A relationship between two people
- An age
- A strongly held belief
- A reason for a change

Any of these could be used by themselves to create entire scenes. Teams could also ask for more than one of them and attempt to combine the suggestions.

Final thoughts

The most important thing to remember when performing these types of events is to keep things genuine. The other elements are just window dressing. Practice time spent working on reality-based improv should be used practicing how to "be real" on-stage. When players can express emotion, they can expand and work on the details. The reality-based scenes are difficult but can be the most rewarding of all the scenes performed.

Exercises in the Games Appendix will help develop skill in this type of event.

Chapter Twenty-One

Other Things to Think About

What about scenes that are a cross between two categories?

There is often some overlap between the events, especially "how" and "what." Many how-style games tell a story as part of their elements. These types of games could be classified as either how events or what events. If teams are playing for a simple, informal performance, it does not really matter (as long as they are entertaining). If a team is playing in a competition, then a decision must be made. How should teams decide how to categorize their scenes?

It comes down to where the team wants to put the emphasis.

If a team decides to tell a western story, they could stress the beginning, middle, and end of the structure and call it a what game. Just as easily, the team could choose to stress the western elements, like the gunfight and rough-looking hero and call it a how game. The team must decide which event their game best fits into.

Teams may wish to consider what other structures they have already created. If a team already has a really good what-type game, then they may wish to make their western into a how game so that they could play them both and exhibit a wider range of talent. Teams must be wary however of pushing the boundaries of their games too far. Often teams will have two very good who-type games and no how or what games. If a competition requires one of each type, the team will sometimes try to turn one of their who games into a how game. Usually this will not work. Most of the time the categories are very different and stress different things. Trying to force round pegs into square holes is not the recipe for quality improv.

How does a team decide what to ask for?

No matter what structures the team ends up presenting, they will have to decide what they want to ask the audience for. These suggestions become the focus for the entire scene, so the team will want to choose them wisely. Teams must make sure that whatever is chosen is something that can be used over and over again. Structures that allow for minimal exploration for one of the ask-fors should be altered to either allow more exploration or to remove the ask-fors. There are some general questions teams should ask themselves when evaluating what to ask for.

Did the suggestion get used throughout the scene?

Some teams get caught asking for two things and using each one for half the scene. This is not ideal. The best structures use all of their suggestions throughout the entire scene. For example, if a team is presenting a talk show with a commercial break of fifteen seconds in the middle, having an ask-for solely for the topic of the commercial would not be desirable — only a small percentage of the scene is used to explore the suggestion.

Did the scene need that many ask-fors?

Teams will at times ask for more suggestions than they need. Showing one suggestion in lots of different ways is easier than attempting to show five different suggestions. In most cases of numerous ask-fors, teams show the first few suggestions well and then rush through a few more — outright omitting a suggestion is the absolute worst-case scenario. Teams should never ask for something if they cannot use it fully.

Does the scene have enough ask-fors?

If a team presents scenes that are too structured (the same jokes are coming out again and again, or the same things are happening every time), then they may wish to ask for more suggestions. Additional suggestions will allow players to perform a more improvised scene. Adding suggestions is not always the cure for a weak structure. Teams may have to drop some of the old ask-fors to get new ones. This rearrangement of suggestions could send the structure in a whole new direction or inspire the team to give the scene a different focus.

Are the ask-fors doing their job?

Do the ask-fors influence significantly every single flag? If a team has a flag which does not change significantly with the suggestions, then either the flags or the suggestions must be altered.

How creative are the ask-fors?

It is by no means required to have creative ask-fors. Teams are fine if they ask for simple suggestions like occupations and locations. Sometimes it can be fun to ask for something unusual. The audience likes teams who stand up and ask for "what you want to be when you grow up" or "the name of your street." Notice that the first example is really asking for an occupation in a creative way. The second is more unusual and could take the scene anywhere (as long as it is used well and not to fill in the blanks).

Part Four
Strategies

Part Four - Strategies

This section is written for and directed at the player. It is an accumulation of ideas that may help a player or team perform well. Included is a list of tips, a method of self-evaluation, how to run an improv show, and what to do before a performance. Hopefully players will have a chance to glance through this material and see what they find important. If there is a problem on the team, they may wish to check this section for a solution.

Chapter Twenty-Two

Tips and Hints

- Make sure that *all* members on your team have performed improv before any competition. This may be done at invitationals, at banquets, even for drama classes. Ensuring that everyone had been on-stage in front of people eases the pre-show jitters. Furthermore, playing games for audiences will give you an indicator of which of your games are most entertaining.
- Read the newspaper/watch the news. Knowledge of current events (even better, a comprehension and insight into them) is often helpful.
- If you have a bad scene during performance, don't let it drain your energy and positive attitude. Rebound and play the next scene with high energy.
- Watch other teams' scenes closely — not only is it fun, but it lets you see what other teams are doing.
- Acquire a broad range of knowledge. Easier said than done, but a player with knowledge, both academic and cultural, is of enormous benefit when the team receives suggestions.
- Smile — convince the audience that you are having fun and it will be infectious for them.
- Know your team and its unique strengths and weaknesses.
- Inspirations for structures and games are all around you. Keep your eyes open.
- Stick with improv — quitters never win.
- Don't expect it all to be easy. The road to success is filled with adversity.
- Do the "little things" in practice. If you make silly mistakes and defend them with, "Well, I would never do that in the show," you're wrong. You will, because you have trained yourself to.
- Nip problems in the bud. Don't let little things blossom into

massive problems in teamwork.
- If you have a problem with a team member, deal with it right away in the open. If you ignore it or talk about it behind their back, nothing will get better and things will get worse.
- Everyone is at different levels/abilities — expect people to have an easier/harder time in some games than others.
- Stage team and personal goals early. Make sure they are compatible.
- Have fun. That's what it is all about.
- Look at improv as a learning experience. Every time you play, review your errors and correct them.
- Evaluate your games after you play them. Say good and bad things. Be specific and constructive. Do not be negative. (It doesn't help to say "that sucked." Better to find out how you would do it better.)
- Go to the games on the nights you don't play. You get to meet new friends, see the games from an audience's perspective, and get to see what else is out there.
- In practice, take turns sitting out of scenes and judging. When you have the ability to know what to look for, you are less likely to make the same mistakes while playing.
- Share the coaching duties. Have different players each take a turn running a practice. They will begin to see what it is like to be on the other end of things. It also gives everyone a chance to show what they are really good at (your good physicalizer can do a practice of physicalizing, etc.). It gives everyone an opportunity to verbalize how they do things.
- Again, smile when you are on-stage. If you are happy, the audience will be happy. Many "judged" events (dance, synchronized swimming, cheerleading) make their competitors smile through the entire event. Take them as your example, but have fun with it.

Chapter Twenty-Three
Self-Evaluation

Sometimes you may wish to judge your performance. Perhaps you are hosting a show with a number of schools (see "Putting on a Show," Chapter Twenty-Four), or maybe you are participating in an organized competition (like the Canadian Improv Games or Theatresports). Depending on the setting, you will be judged on different things. Here are some categories that may be evaluated and the things that the judges will normally look for.

Rules of the stage

Did the team

- Play at the front of the stage?
- Spread out on the stage?
- Balance the stage?
- Use levels?
- Face the audience?
- "Mug" the audience?
- Talk in clear voices?
- Speak so that they could be heard by the entire audience?
- Avoid speaking over each other?
- Appear to be confident on-stage?

Physicalization

Did the team

- Show a where?
- Create an interesting where?
- Physicalize the unique qualities of their environment?
- Avoid destroying a where that was already created?
- Physicalize with mime?
- Physicalize with people as background objects?
- Physicalize with players as foreground objects?
- Physicalize in a manner related to the suggestion?
- Use levels in their physicalization?
- Physicalize in a manner that augmented the rest of the scene?

Use of suggestion

Did the team

- Use the suggestion?
- Use the suggestion in a manner that only that suggestion could be used?
- Use the suggestion throughout the scene?
- Use ideas that are related to the suggestion (bananas when the suggestion is monkey)?
- Do more than just plug the suggestion into blanks?
- Not let their structure overshadow their suggestion?
- Genuinely improvise the scene?
- Explore the unique characteristics of the suggestion?
- Let the suggestion influence one or more of the who, what, where, when, why, or hows?

Rules of improvisation

- Did the team avoid the improvisation downfalls described in Chapter Three (blocking, wimping, etc.)?
- Did the team explore fully what they were attempting to explore (be it characterization, storytelling, or style portrayal, etc.)
- Characterization: Were the characters unique, well-developed, and fully explored?
- Storytelling: Did the scene tell a real story or was it just a series of events?
- Style portrayal: Did the team explore all of the elements of the style they were attempting?
- Vignettes: Did the team explore their suggestion in a variety of settings? Were their different choices really different or just superficial repetitions?
- Scenarios: Did the team really explore the scenario and the whys behind it, or did they just touch upon its surface? If they were attempting genuine emotion, was it really genuine or was it melodramatic and fake?

The structure

- Did the structure help the team to improvise or did it hinder their attempts?

- Did the flags use the suggestion or just mention it? Or not use it at all?
- Did the team succeed without even using flags? (If so, great — more points!)
- Was the structure slightly different than what had been done before?
- Was the structure unique (very different) from before?

Teamwork

Did the team

- Work together to create the scene?
- Help each other to make things flow smoothly?
- Have background players help those in the lead by feeding in the scene?
- Have foreground players help each other by feeding each other?
- Use the offers each of the other players gave?
- Watch and listen to what was happening in the scene? If things were going badly, did someone get in and help? If things were going well, did people stay out unless helpful?
- Avoid taking attention away from the people who should be having it?

Is that it?

No. Improv scenes tend to be more than the sum of their parts. All of these elements will help you create a good scene, but in the end it is best to judge scenes holistically. Beyond the use of suggestion elements and some improv foundation skills, just about anyone will be able to differentiate a good scene from a bad one or an entertaining one from a dull one. This list will just help you realize why one scene was better than another.

Chapter Twenty-Four

Putting on a Show

After you have spent all this time improving your improv skills, it is time you put on a show. We will concern ourselves with two possibilities. Either you are a high school group who is looking to put on a show at your school, or you are planning to participate in some sort of improv competition (like the Canadian Improv Games). Our recommendation is that you always attempt to put on your own show before you try to play in a competitive setting. Non-threatening performances are one of the best ways to test your games, your skills under pressure, and your ability to handle an audience. It also provides an excellent opportunity to gain performance experience, to gain confidence, to create awareness of your team within your school, and to try out new or risky (difficult) games. The more times you perform for an audience, the better your team will be.

How do we run our own show?

There are a number of things you have to get done before putting on your own show.

Get known
Before putting on a full show, you may wish to get yourself recognized around the school. Try to get your team thrown in as part of other assemblies. Doing one scene as part of a spirit assembly, coffee house, or talent show is a lot less intimidating than holding down a full show without support.

Get permission to do a show
In most schools, permission is a simple matter of letting the head of the drama department or someone on the administrative staff know that you wish to do a show. You might be required to have a teacher supervisor for the show. Make sure you find a teacher as soon as possible. The organization of the show is up to you.

Decide when to have your show

It is recommended that your first full show be done over a lunch hour. This demands much less organization than after-school shows. This way your team will only need to prepare a few games (four or five), and your audience is already at school with an hour of free time. A show can also be done for another class in the school. If you can get permission to do it, many students may appreciate the break you give them from their normal classes (a drama teacher may be interested in having an improv show for their class). One team once arranged that anyone who paid two dollars got out of their second-period class to come watch their show. In any case, you will want to think which day of the week is best for your school. Mondays might not be a good idea because everyone has had the weekend to forget that there is a show. Find out what other school events are happening. Make sure your show does not conflict with something that will steal your audience. Try to decide at least a week in advance what day and at what time your performance will be.

Decide where to have your show

You can hold a show anywhere there is enough room for a playing area and an audience. Drama studios, gymnasiums, lecture halls, an auditorium or even the cafeteria, are all possible places to perform. Choose your performance space (if you have a choice) and reserve it as soon as you can.

Publicity

You need an audience to do a show. It is your job to make the school aware of your show. The most popular way to do this is with posters. Make sure posters are legible and contain all the important information: what the show is, when the show is, where the show is. You might need to get the posters approved by the administration or a department head before putting them up. Another way to notify the student body is through the morning or afternoon announcements. Again, make sure your announcement contains all the important information. Word of mouth is very effective as well; tell all your friends and make sure they come.

The show

What you put in your show is up to you. If the show is at lunch hour or before school or immediately after school, then you can likely only fit five or six games. You should have at least four games to show. If your team is doing an evening performance, then you will want to have a much bigger repertoire of games.

*It is highly recommended that only more advanced teams try to have an evening show that does not involve other teams. It is very hard for one team to entertain an audience for up to two hours (including intermissions). Any team that attempts this must have many **different types of games** in their repertoire, good stamina, experience in handling an audience, and abundant improv skill.*

When practicing for the show, keep in mind that you can change the order and content of your show at any time. If a game starts to feel stale or does not work, throw it aside for the moment and do something else for the show. A good idea is to start and end with stronger games.

Charging money

It is not necessary to charge admission to a small lunch-hour show. However, if an after-school show costs you money to put on, then most students should be willing to pay a dollar or two.

Warming up the audience

It is possible that there are people in the audience who have no clue who you are or what you are doing. Your audience might not know the rules and boundaries of improv. They might not realize how important they are to the show! You want your audience to understand, appreciate, and enjoy your performance. You want good suggestions from an audience that is not afraid to yell them out. That is why it is important to warm up your audience.

A warm-up should be short, energetic and include a brief explanation of what you are doing. For example:

"Hello everyone, we are (insert name of team here) and we are going to be doing some improv. How many people have seen improv before? None. Great. Well, what we do is make up scenes based on your suggestions — so we need your help. Whenever we ask for a suggestion, feel free to yell some out. For example, I might ask for a location and you would all say ... (Hopefully someone will yell suggestions here.) Wow, that was awful. Try again. Let's say I needed an occupation ... (more suggestions). Better. What if I wanted a characteristic? (Everyone yells.) Good. Please, when giving suggestions, keep in mind that it's a family show."

Another good idea for a team performing for an audience not familiar with this style of improv is to have a short introduction before each game explaining the game and giving examples of what kind of suggestions you need. For example:

"Our next game is a story-type game. In this game we tell the story of how someone becomes famous. What we need from you is a famous celebrity like Tina Turner or George Clooney and a location, like a supermarket or the library."

This explains a little further what they are about to see and helps them understand what kind of suggestions you need.

Getting suggestions

You can get your own suggestions from your audience. You know what will work well, you know the suggestions you need. Do not take suggestions you have already practiced.

After the show

Do not forget to thank your audience. Make sure you leave the room in the state you found it. Within the first few days after the show, your team should have a meeting to discuss what was good and bad about the show. Try to be honest and objective. Learn from your mistakes.

Other shows

Your school could use your team in student council events such as a lunchtime event. The team can do fundraising shows for the grad committee or perform in the school fashion show. If you can, get involved in school activities. Anything can be a venue for improv, and the more shows your team has under their belt, the better you will do in competition.

Customizing shows

The great thing about improv is that it is flexible. Perhaps you will be asked to do a show for a specific school event or even for a community, government, school board, or corporate event. You can adjust your show to fit the needs of your audience or requirements. For example, maybe your school's grad committee is having a talent show one night to raise money for graduation. Your team could make up some games based around your school's graduates, i.e., a prom date character game and a getting-to-the-prom story game.

Some things you may wish to note

Know who your audience is and what the event is. Find out who the main people involved with the event are and some characteristics or notable things about them. Find out some information surrounding the event. For instance, if you are to perform at a fundraising event for a new community center and you know that the mayor is a really good line dancer and that the construction crew for the building is being difficult, you can use these bits in your scenes. You can even base a game around this information. People are delighted to recognize things about themselves in the scenes. Do not use insulting or offensive material. (Consider your audience — a show at a senior citizen home might have to be more traditional and conservative.)

What about getting other schools involved?

Hosting a night of improv is a great way to meet teams from other schools, learn from each other, and have lots of fun. Hosting this type of event takes more planning.

Permission

First you need to talk to someone on the administration staff about having a show. You will probably need teacher supervision. You might even need two or three teachers. Each team will probably need to bring their own teacher supervisor. You might have to pay the custodians to stay late. You will likely have to end the show and have everyone out by 11:00 p.m. These are all things to discuss.

When

Decide on the date several weeks in advance. This way you can send out invitations and get replies well before the show date. Seven o'clock is a good starting time. It gives the other teams time to eat dinner and get to your school.

Where

You will need a bigger space to accommodate more teams and the audience. An auditorium, gym, a large cafeteria, or a large lecture hall would be big enough.

Who

You can host a night with only two teams. It is much more fun to have four or five teams playing. If you have any more than six then it becomes difficult to play more than two games each. You will want a host or referee and a timekeeper for the evening. These should be people who know what improv is all about. It is not necessary to have judges. If you want judges, they should not score each scene but rather give awards for "best line," "best moment," "best scene," etc. Perhaps these judges can be the teacher supervisors from visiting schools.

If you have someone available who knows improv really well, you may wish to use them as an adjudicator. They can fill in the teams at the end of the show on what they did well and what they need to work on.

What

If you have four to six teams competing, you should be able to fit three rounds. If you have more than that, you can likely only do two. If you have fewer teams, you can play four rounds. Teams can bring their own structures or just wing it. We recommend having a mandatory vignette or vignette-type game and two (or three) other games of the teams' choosing. Note: It can be fun to mix the players from all the teams up for part or all of the night. Especially if nobody has brought game structures with them, mixing teams is a great idea.

125

Publicity/Invitations

You will need to make invitations and send them out two weeks in advance. To ensure you will have commitments, you might want to set a small entrance fee and include with the invitation a confirmation sheet that the team must sign and return to you with the entrance fee.

Publicity is the same as before only you can have other teams make posters for their schools. Anyone from any school is welcome to watch, but they have to know about the show in order to come.

How does a competition differ?

A lot of your hard work may come down to one or two nights of competition. It is important to be at your optimal level of performance for these nights. Do everything you can to relax and enjoy the experience.

The night before

If your team is playing on a Friday night, the Thursday night is extremely important. You should ensure that you get to bed at a reasonable hour and obtain a good night's sleep. Improv demands vitality and energy; staying out the night before your performance will leave your body and mind too drained to perform at a quality level.

Performance day

Performance day is of critical importance to guarantee a positive experience. Make sure to eat a nutritious breakfast and lunch — nobody wants to be short of energy for the performance. Game day nervousness and worry are common for many participants in other arts or sports fields — improv players are no different. Generally, a relaxing day is of great value. Do not get stressed out about insignificant sources of irritation. Avoid things that will distract you from focusing on participation. Some players or teams even have certain routines or rituals. Anything that helps you focus on the performance is a good thing.

Once school has ended, you may choose to meet together at the school, house, or elsewhere to hang out and discuss any strategies for the night. Remember to use this time to eat a good meal — it is easy to forget in the excitement. Many teams also head together to the venue for the improv show. Allow yourself enough time to commute to the venue without having to rush — the stress of being late for the show adds an unnecessary burden on anyone playing.

At the venue

Teams usually arrive at the venue approximately two hours before show time. Upon the arrival of all the teams, organizers of the tournament will probably run some sort of vocal, physical, and improvisational warm-up. Actively participate in these exercises — organizers are most likely specialists and are masters of getting teams excited to perform.

Any improv competition offers incredible and unique opportunities for players to meet and interact with others in a friendly, open, and non-threatening manner. Take advantage of this opportunity to meet students and coaches from other schools — performing can be a lot more fun in front of friends; why not make a number of new ones to enhance your comfort level when competing?

Hopefully some free time will be offered for teams to discuss any last-minute strategies, plans, or tidbits of wisdom. Avoid dissension in the ranks and try to remain a cohesive group. Be careful about changing too much at the last minute. Sometimes changing a structure at this time can work (especially for teams who have not read this book ☺), but in general, stick with what you know. Trust your coach and trust in yourselves to do a good job. And above all, do not be intimidated by the skill you perceive the other teams to have. No matter how good they look, they are probably thinking the same thing about you.

For your entire time backstage it is important to be attentive. Take time to listen to the organizers. The organizers will be giving directions, schedules, and other possible changes. Being an attentive audience is of great benefit.

This is also your final opportunity to check the appropriateness of your attire. Improvisational performance is a physical event, and players may be unexpectedly called upon to create a whirring chain saw, a fuming dragon, or anything else frantic and fast. Safety and practicality are the key concerns with wardrobe choices. Anything on your person which is dangling may be a potential source of danger, from pieces of clothing to large hoop earrings, necklaces, or other pieces of jewelry. Players wearing low-cut shirts, skirts, or kilts may run the risk of exposing more than just their improv ability! Shoes, ideally a pair with decent support, should be tied with no dangling laces.

Time to go!

Well, finally, here it comes — lights, crowds, the excitement of the big show. Moments before the show begins, the teams will be gathered to enter. The referee and the timekeeper of the event will enter onto the stage and prepare the audience for the show in the form of a brief speech. During this time, teams, standing in silence, are waiting backstage. The referee or timekeeper will introduce the team and the audience will applaud. At this point, the team runs out, exploding in a flourish of energy. Keep in mind that the introduction will be the audience's first impression of the team. Most of the time a team will just run out, yell and cheer, and then sit down in their defined spot. Some teams will make mini-presentations (such as a brief cheer or dance), but in order to keep the show to a reasonable schedule, these introductions should be extremely brief (five seconds or less). The team will then take their seats in the predetermined area of the stage while the next team is introduced.

Showtime!

The referee will call the teams one by one onto the stage to present their games. Be ready to go at any time (even if you think you are not next). If the referee does call your team, jump up excitedly and enthusiastically. If the performance involves getting a suggestion out of a hat or other container, have a person designated to pick one. This preplanning avoids two potentially awkward scenes — having no one come forward for the suggestion, making the team look forgetful or unorganized, or having several people come forward for the suggestion, making the team look

128

divisive and uncooperative. For the other types of games, in which suggestions are solicited from the audience, have the person(s) asking the question predetermined. Moreover, ensure that the questions have been practiced in a polished form and are correct — you do not want Marv saying, "Hello, I'd like an object, please," and having Marv's team say, "No, we want an occupation!" After the scene is over, have everyone on the team congratulate each other and smile at the audience. You do not want to come out of a scene in a down mood — it does not help your energy for the next scene and no one in the audience (including the judges) wants to see you sulking. Treat every scene you do as if it was the best one you have ever done. Finally, any props or blocks that were moved or scattered around the stage during the scene should be returned to (approximately) their starting positions.

During other scenes

While watching the scenes of other teams, show some respect. Treat the performances of the other teams as you would have them treat yours. Be courteous, supportive, and interested. Above all, refrain from criticizing, commenting, or dissecting the scene while it is being presented. This is time for you to watch and enjoy the talent of the other teams. Do not use this time to argue about things you may have disliked about your own scenes. Likewise, do not discuss any plans for your upcoming scenes. Stay focused on what you are doing, not what happened or what is coming up.

Scores

You may receive a score for the scenes you perform. Often a team of judges will score every event. In some cases their scores may decide which teams will move on to finals or receive trophies. Obviously not all teams will advance to the next round — some teams will make finals and other teams will not. But improv is really about cooperation and fun. When scores are announced, **do not** listen attentively. Hum or cover your ears. When scores are announced, be happy. Be happy for yourselves, for your co-improvians, and for the spirit of cooperative competition. Expect high scores and you are setting yourself up for disappointment — do not worry about scores and you will be ecstatic with the results.

129

Love improv! Have fun! Cooperate with others; compete with yourself! Cheer for other teams! Cheer for the officials! Cheer for the judges! Make the most of your experience! Go to shows you are not involved in — it will give you a broader improv background and will let you get to know lots of great people! Most importantly ... *have fun!*

Appendices

This section includes all of the material that did not logically flow through the rest of the manual. Included are specialized sections like competing in the Canadian Improv Games or learning how to sing and rhyme on the spot. Also included are a large number of games and lists and a two week lesson plan which utilizes some of them. Finally this section ends with an annotated bibliography and a glossary of improv terms. It is our intention that while the core of this manual teaches everything one would need to know about improv, it is these appendices that will be used on a daily basis.

Improv Games Events

What is this section all about?

The Canadian Improv Games is a charitable not-for-profit organization founded in 1977 that teaches improvisation through cooperative competition. Many teams reading this book are (or some day will be) participants in their games. If you are part of a high school and wish to become part of the Canadian Improv Games (whether you live in Canada or not) or even start your own regional organization please call 1-613-726-6339 or check out their webite at www.improv.ca. The CIG have trademaked all their materials, so please don't use any of it without permission (just call them and ask nicely).

This section briefly describes the rules. It also breaks down each event and gives some of the authors' personal interpretations of how they are best performed.

The Rules of the CIG

These games have only a few rules that must be followed. Teams must be composed entirely of players from the same high school. There is a maximum of eight players on a team. Props may be used, but must be made available to the other teams playing (with the exception of musical instruments). All of the scenes performed are to be a maximum of four minutes (warnings are given when there is one minute, thirty seconds, and ten seconds remaining). Teams must play the two required events and two of the three optional events.

The Events of the CIG

We have chosen to describe each event in five categories:

The Rules

Our interpretation of the rules for the event. These are quite vague and open-ended. However, any time you are confused, look back at these core rules for what is really important.

Overview

This is a more specific interpretation of the rules to help you get on the right track.

The Game

Here we list some ideas for how you can set up your game. This section includes examples of what some teams have done in the past and what some of your options are.

Be Careful

In this section we list some things to watch out for. Some of the things you should be thinking about when you are evaluating how you set up your structure. There are very few rules in improv games and often the best teams succeed by breaking the "accepted doctrine." However if you are going to do something very different, there are still things you need to "be careful" about.

Common Errors

While there are thousands of right ways to do things there are millions of wrong ways. Every year you will learn from the mistakes you made the year before. In this section we list some of the common errors made by many teams in the past so that you can avoid making the same ones. Hopefully teams will continue to learn from each other and the overall level of play will improve every year.

How Do I Structure this Game?

Our structuring section has many helpful hints for all of the improv game events. This section sends you looking in the right place and gives some of the differences between official improv game style and our categories.

The Story Event

The Rules

The team must design and play an original structure that demonstrates its ability to perform a story. The structure must not overshadow the teams' ability to improvise. The team must solicit suggestions from the audience and use them to develop their scene.

Overview

The story game focuses on the *what*. The *what* consists of the events and actions that occur in your story. The story game is plot-driven. It must have a beginning, middle, and end.

The Game

There are many different ways of telling a story. A common choice is through narrative, but you should not feel limited to this option. A story could be told through dance, mime, song, poetry, art, or movement. The story game is a very open game and we challenge you to push its boundaries.

It is possible to take an existing story and change it using your suggestions. For example, you might use *Goldilocks and the Three Bears*, and ask for an occupation and a location. Now we can have "Goldilocks and the Three Lion Tamers Who Live on the Moon." You can tell a story of a person's first date, or get someone from the audience to recall a moment in their life for you to replay with suggestions.

Equally effective is creating a new story from scratch. You may want to ask for a story title and tell the story that follows. Maybe an existing story could be used as a starting point and you tell what happens before or after the well-known events. Another possibility is to tell a story from an unusual point of view, for example, Mike's first taste of bubble gum from the gum's point of view.

Be Careful

Most stories (with some exceptions) have a well-developed format of rising action followed by a climax and ending with a denouement (see the Storytelling section of Chapter Four for more details). If your story does not have these sections be very careful and make doubly sure you are still telling a story.

Common Errors

Some story games are told as a series of unrelated events. If you ask for an object and two locations and then show the object being used in each of those two locations you may have told two different stories, but you did not meet the criteria for this game. There is nothing wrong with exploring different locations in a story game, just make sure you are still telling a coherent and interconnected story.

How Do I Structure this Event?

Use the "What" category as your base.

The Style Event

The Rules
The team must design and play an original structure that demonstrates its ability to recreate and perform a style of the performing arts or literature. The structure must not overshadow the teams' ability to improvise. The team must solicit suggestions from the audience and use them to develop their scene.

Overview
The style game focuses on the *how*. The *how* is the manner in which the story is told or how the information of the scene is conveyed. A style is any method of presenting or expressing the story or information. A style is a form of presentation that has numerous examples and definite characteristics that make it unique. The style game is driven by the characteristics of the style you have chosen.

The Game
Most teams choose a style and then have suggestions modify how they will present it. By choosing a style you are effectively deciding the manner in which your story or information will be presented. You can then get suggestions that will decide what you will present. One way of doing this is to ask for an existing story and present it in your style. For example, the team could do an opera and ask for a story title or do news coverage and ask for a fairy tale.

The suggestions you ask for depend on your style. If you are doing the style of a children's pop-up book, then you might want to ask for a children's story. Another option would be to take something very foreign to the matter normally presented by the style. The same pop-up book structure could be done asking for a current news event.

Be Careful
Not everything is a style! While no firm definition of what exactly constitutes a style exists, you should be able to identify at least three examples of the style. An action movie is a style, but the film *Rambo* is not a style. Playwright William Shakespeare, author

James Joyce, and filmmaker Stanley Kubrick are among the very few who have impacted popular culture to create their own style. Not sure if an idea fits as a style? Ask a teacher, expert, or someone in your regional improv tournament.

To further illustrate what we mean by style, consider the style of Shakespearean tragedy. There are many examples of this style: *Romeo and Juliet, Macbeth, King Lear,* and *Hamlet* to name just a few. Some of its elements are the tragic hero, iambic pentameter, and dark foreshadowing. Note that *Romeo and Juliet* exists within Shakespearean tragedy and is *not* by itself a style.

Make sure you do some research on your style so that you know all of its elements. If you do not know a style well you will have trouble showing it effectively in an improvised setting. The better you know your style the more likely you are to be faithful to it. If the style you are doing is an unusual one, be prepared to explain to the audience and judges the elements of your style before you even begin to get suggestions.

Common Errors

The most common error in style games is not doing a style. If you do any style beyond those listed in the appendix you may wish to check with your tournament organizers to make sure that what you are doing really is a style.

Another common mistake is telling the audience your style is one thing and then doing something else. If you say your style is family sitcom, do not just do a remake of a *Cosby Show* episode. There are many common elements of the family sitcom style, so make sure you are exploring them and not working through one case. In general if you have set characters in your structure (like Bill Cosby and his family) then you are not doing a style.

How Do I Structure this Event?

Use the "How" category as a base. A style is really just a genre taken from some sort of media.

The Character Event

The Rules

The team must design and play an original structure that demonstrates its ability to portray a character. The structure must not overshadow the teams' ability to improvise. The team must solicit suggestions from the audience and use them to develop their scene.

Overview

The character game focuses on the *who*. The *who* are the characters in the scene. What makes them special? How do they relate with other people? How do they affect the scene? How do they react in different situations? Do they make things happen? The character game is obviously character driven.

The Game

A common choice of ask-for is a character trait. Another option would be to use an existing character such as a celebrity or a character from a book or movie and place them in unfamiliar circumstances. Some teams have based characters on animals, magazines, or physical objects they receive from the audience.

Regardless of how or from what suggestion you get your character there is always something that makes the character unique. That something is the characteristic. This characteristic is what makes things happen in your scene. If the scene is about how a character lost their job then they lose the job because of their characteristic.

Be Careful

Do not let your character game drift away from your showing of character. Just because you ask for a characteristic does not mean you are automatically following the rules of the Character game. Remember to keep your focus on the character. Every suggestion you ask for should be used as a vehicle to show the characters you have created. Whatever happens, do not let players who are not the "characters" take focus away from the players who are.

Common Errors

If you ask for too many characteristics you may have difficulty showing them all. Remember that you only have four minutes and you want to explore each character as much as possible. Do not be afraid to make your characters too big (there is no such thing). The Character game is not for "small" characters.

How Do I Structure this Event?

Use the "Who" section as a base.

The Theme Event

The Rules

The team must design and play an original structure that demonstrates its ability to explore one or more aspects of a theme. The structure must not overshadow the teams' ability to improvise. The team is given the theme by the referees but may solicit suggestions from the audience and use them to develop their scene.

Overview

The theme game focuses on exploration. The team should use their knowledge of whos, whats, wheres, whens, whys, and hows to show the various aspects of the given theme. How does the theme change when looked at from a different angle? How does the theme change when one of the Ws is changed? Exploring the theme does not mean doing a lot of scenes, it means showing the theme either in different ways, in different settings, or with different characters.

The Game

A common choice for the theme game is to perform a vignette. A vignette is a series of short sketches similar to the freeze game (page 219). This allows the team to show the theme in many different ways very quickly and efficiently. Most theme games are done this way or in a slight variation thereof. Look at the freeze game for some possibilities.

Another option teams have chosen is to set the theme game in a certain location and have different things happen which relate to the theme. Various characters could enter the scene and influence its direction in a manner related to the suggestion. A similar method takes a set character and observes a day in their life where the theme takes a significant role in a variety of different ways.

Regardless of your choice the theme should be explored under changes in one or more of the who, what, where, when, why, and how.

Be Careful

Exploring the theme does not mean doing lots of scenes. You

should strive to look at different aspects of the theme and not repeat the same ones over and over with superficial changes. Here's an example: The theme is competition. Having players come out in twos to perform scenes over and over where they are both competing to do something better than the other is not exploring the theme of competition. This is true even if they are competing to do different things. Instead try to show the different aspects of competition (the good winner, the bad winner, the sore loser, the benefits of competition, the problems with competition, the lack of competition, when a competitive person and non-competitive person meet, etc.).

Common Errors

Make sure you are showing your theme and not just saying it. Puns do not help you show the theme. Saying the word does not help either. It is better to show the audience your use of the theme than it is to explain it to them in words. Trust in your ability to show the audience what you are doing, and trust in your audience to figure things out. You are doing no one any favors by saying "Wow! You are sure a good competitor!" Remember, *show* don't *tell.*

If you are doing an "alternative" theme game (meaning one that is not set up like the vignette) be sure that it explores the theme in different ways. These formats are entertaining, because they are something different, but be sure that it helps you explore and does not hinder you. Some things to watch for are:

- Does it limit the number of players that can help do the exploring?
- Do you often come up with ideas that cannot be used due to the nature of the structure?
- Is it sometimes slow-moving or does it have large segments where the theme is not being explored?
- Does it spend a large amount of time touching on one aspect of the theme without really exploring it in depth or showing a different aspect?

How Do I Structure this Event?

Use the Use-of-Suggestion chapter as a base. In the past, official improv suggestions for this game have always been broad concepts. Take a look at the Appendix of Lists for some example themes from previous years. We have also included some more exotic examples as the improv games are constantly changing and your team should be ready for anything.

The Life Event

The Rules

The team must create an original scene that demonstrates its ability to portray a pivotal moment in someone's life. Any emotion expressed or actions or reactions shown in the scene must be genuine. Any structure used must not overshadow the team's ability to improvise. The team will solicit suggestions from the audience and use them to create their scene.

Overview

The issues game focuses on the *why*. The *why* is the meaning behind the events that are taking place. What is happening? Why is it happening? Who is the scenario affecting? Why is it important? What was the background of the situation? What are its future effects? Why should the characters in the scene care? How are the characters in the scene related? The live event is the "real" event. It can be funny but should not be played for laughs. It can be serious but should not be played for melodrama. Lots of things can happen in the scenario, but everything should be genuine.

The Game

The life game is generally played as a straight scenario. After being given their suggestion the team decides in their huddle on the who, what, and where for the scene and performs the moment for the audience's pleasure. The best of these scenes are those that are performed empathetically as if the players were in that situation. Melodrama and slapstick comedy have no place in the life event.

Other options are possible (and desirable) if done genuinely. Scenes have been done with the players being clowns or performing a ballad. These choices are fine as long as the feelings portrayed and actions presented are genuine and real.

Be Careful

Being genuine does not mean crying. It does not mean yelling. It does not mean showing extreme emotions. It means acting in such a way that what you are doing seems real. Dealing with major life issues is *not* required in this event. Just because the event involves a moment in someone's life does not mean that moment has to be one involving anorexia, suicide, abortion, or abuse. These are valid topics if shown in a real and genuine manner, but it is equally valid to show the breakup of a relationship, the loss of a friend, or the achievement of a surprising success. Showing your range is good, but forcing a range into a scene where it does not belong can be hazardous to your scene's success.

Remember that you must show genuine, real people on stage. It cannot be said enough. The easiest way to do that is to play yourself or someone close to you. Imagine yourself in the situation given and what you would do. Failing that, it is easiest to play someone your own age. You know how your peers talk and act more than anyone else. If you attempt to play someone significantly different than you in attitude or age it is much more difficult. Playing an adult or young child is very difficult even for the most experienced actor. If you choose to have a character like this in your scene, beware. Be particularly cautious about putting such an adult or child as your main character(s) in a scene. Playing someone different than yourself is allowed, but *be careful.*

Common Errors

Do not shoot yourself in the foot with your choice of ask-for. Think of possible suggestions you could be given for your ask-for and be sure they will allow you to explore the scene in a genuine way. If you ask for "an event from someone's life," you could get "retirement." It may be difficult for the players to deal with an issue from which they are so far removed in a genuine way. A better ask-for might be "an event that could happen to someone in high school." That way, they will be able to really explore the suggestion they are given.

If your team chooses to ask for a scenario, make sure you are not just replaying the scenario given. Remember that the audience has already heard what was said. It is up to you to explore the whys related to the scenario and not act out the action that was spoken. For example, if the scenario was "you have broken up with your boy/girlfriend," do not show the breakup. Show what happened immediately after the breakup, or a week later, or a year later.

145

Explore the scenario, do not repeat it. No matter what the suggestion is, the team must pay attention and listen to its details. Teams sometimes forget the suggestion and go off in the wrong direction. In the worst cases, teams have overstructured their game to the point where they are trying to force their structure into a scenario where it does not fit. Make sure you play the suggestion you are given.

In general the teams that do not do the life event right go one of two ways with their problems. Either the scene is played for comedy with players playing caricatures (of their own creation or directly off *Saturday Night Live*), or the scene is played as a melodrama where the main character has one or more huge problems. Teams have trouble finding the right balance to play a scene real. The key is to stop acting so hard and just play the scene. You act real in 99% of your life, it is just a matter of taking that reality and putting it onto the stage.

How Do I Structure this Event?

Use the reality-based chapter (page 98) as a base. One way to practice these scenes is just to play scenarios. Check out the list of scenarios in the appendix and try playing them in a real and genuine manner.

Practice Schedule

With the games that follow in Appendix Two, it is quite simple to put together detailed lesson plans. Just teach a little of the theory from the appropriate chapter and then jump right into the games that teach those skills. What follows here are a few sample lesson plans which can help you get started.

The plans have been designed for five classes at an hour and a half each. Each class can easily be expanded by adding more games (the better option) or teaching more theory. By speeding things up the classes can be taught in an hour.

Plan 1: Improv Introduction

Lesson 1: Improv Basics
Theory: Improv Foundations 1, 2, and 3
Games: Blocking, Yes and ..., and their variations

Lesson 2: Physicalization
Theory: Review last class, stressing Rules of the Stage. Physicalizing
Games: Creating Locations, People and Objects, Miming

Lesson 3: Characterization
Theory: Characterization
Games: Character Walk, Gibberish Interview, Character Monolog, Opening the Box, Pop-Machine

Lesson 4: Storytelling
Theory: Storytelling
Games: Breaking Routines, Phrase at a Time

Lesson 5: Use of Suggestion
Theory: Use of Suggestion
Games: The Object, Desert Island

Plan 2: Improv Skill Work

Lesson 1: Feeding and Teamwork
Theory: Teamwork (Feeding), Characterization (Feeding), Sharing Focus
Games: Hot Dog Stand, focus games

Lesson 2: Raising the Stakes
Theory: Teamwork (Adding to the scene)
Games: Raising the Stakes, review games

Lesson 3: The Who, What and Where
Theory: Who, What, Where, and The Huddle
Games: Practice huddles with scenarios, short (fifteen-second) scenes with a who, what, and where.

Lesson 4: Theme Game
Theory: Review Storytelling, Theme Event Structuring
Games: Freeze (add themes), Vignette Theme Game (use techniques from Theme event structuring)

Lesson 5: Structuring
Theory: Structuring (Flags)
Games: Design games in groups of four to eight with flags. Each group given a style

Appendix Three

Games

This appendix contains a series of games divided into **warm-up** games, **exercises**, and **practice games**. Each game is described in the same format:

Type of game: Warm-up, exercise, or practice, also what specific skill the game works on.

Purpose: Precisely what the game is meant to improve.

Group size: How many players are used in the game at one time.

Duration: How much time should be spent on the game (or once through the game).

Description: How to play the game.

Notes: Hints on playing the game. Things to watch out for. Common problems. The aspects which should be stressed.

Variations: Slight variations on the game through to different games which teach the same concept.

Games List

All Together Now

Type of Game: Warm-up

Purpose: To get the team to listen to each other and increase the teamwork and cooperation skills of the group.

Group Size: The entire team

Duration: Ten minutes

Description

The team wanders around the room aimlessly. At any point someone will freeze. Any player who notices the frozen player should also freeze. Thus, the entire team ends up in a frozen point; once this occurs, the players begin walking around the room again, until someone freezes again. This game sounds quiet easy, but cutting the reaction time of the team can be quite challenging.

Notes

In this game, players should act as they would in a performance — loud people talking loudly and quiet people talking quietly — this will help make the game a better simulation of how the team works together as a unit than if people try to act differently from their usual mannerisms.

Variations

1. With noise — Have the players speak or make noises as they walk around. Adding sound to the game gives the players more things to concentrate on. **2. Sitting** — Have the players sit around the room in random positions. Everyone closes their eyes. Every player begins to talk or make sounds. A player at random will stop, and when they do, other players must notice the absence of the person's voice and once a player has done so, they themselves will stop making noise. This becomes more challenging if some players make noises, others speak in words, or if players vary their volume.

Count Together

Type of Game: Warm-up
Purpose: To develop the ability to work together as a team
Group Size: The entire team. The bigger the group, the harder the game.
Duration: A long time when you start, but it gets easier

Description

The team stands in a circle. Everyone closes their eyes. Someone will say "one." Another person on the team will say "two." When two people say a number at the same time, the group resets its count and begins again at one. The team keeps trying to count higher and higher. There is no set pattern — players speak when they feel they should. The game is easiest when people do not rush and allow themselves a long time.

Notes

This is a great game for team unity and synergy. It will help players relax, and take their minds off other problems. It should force them to concentrate on a team goal.

Expect the team to have difficulty at first. In the beginning it is hard even counting to ten. If the game is played periodically, the team will most likely demonstrate a marked improvement.

If some players are speaking a disproportionate number of times, add the rule that no person may say a number twice in a row, or until two (or three or four or five …) people have said something. As a coach you may wish to mess up the game if the team starts trying "tricks" (Like going through all the numbers in a circle pattern). There should be no obvious communication.

Variations

1. **Lying on the ground** — The team lies on the ground, strewn about the room randomly. Eyes are closed. It may help the team focus. 2. **Count down** — The team may try counting down from a number. 3. **Alphabet counting** — Letters of the alphabet are used instead of numbers. 4. **Word-at-a-time** — Instead of numbers, insert the Word-at-a-time game, each player says a word, and other players say a word which joins the previous words in the telling of a story.

Cross Circle

Type of Game: Warm-up

Purpose: To increase players' abilities to react to the actions of their teammates

Group Size: The entire team

Duration: Five minutes

Description

Have the team stand up in a fairly large circle. One person, Player A, selects a random person in the circle and calls out, "Hi, B." Then, Player A walks towards Player B. Before Player A walks into and collides with Player B, Player B selects at random another person and calls out "Hi, C." Player B then walks towards Player C. Player C then selects another Player in the circle and calls "Hi, D" and walks towards Player D. At this point, Player A has probably reached Player B's original spot. Player A stops moving and waits to be called upon by another player. Maintaining the pattern is the point of the game. The first time this game is played, the team should walk very slowly, so that the team masters the pattern and more importantly, avoids accidental collisions.

Notes

Everyone has to be watching all the time — the game grinds to a frustrating standstill when even one player is napping.

Variations

1. Pointing — Instead of calling to people, have each player signal their desired target by pointing. This use of a less obvious signal forces players to pay more attention to small movements.
2. Winking — To increase the difficulty even more, have players use a more subtle cue, such as winking. **3. Word-at-a-time** — If the team has mastered the game, and finds minimal challenge even when increasing speed, have them combine it with Word-at-a-time, where instead of calling out "Hi" or using signals, the players utter a word.

Hand Pressure

Type of Game: Warm-up

Purpose: This warm-up is to get the team all working together and listening with their bodies as well as their ears.

Group Size: The entire team

Duration: Five minutes

Description

The team stands up in a circle with everyone holding hands. One player squeezes one of the hands that they are holding. The recipient of the squeeze then squeezes the hand of the other person whose hand they are holding. Each player receiving a squeeze keeps squeezing the hand of the other person with whom they are holding hands. A surge of squeezing should run through the circle. Players should refrain from commenting when they receive a squeeze (they should also not make extraneous body movements). This keeps the squeeze "anonymous" — players have no idea when or from which direction they will receive a squeeze.

Notes

Improv is fast-paced and reactionary. Any game which features the reception of a stimulus and then some action in response is always a great way to help players get their reflexes going.

Variations

1. Multiple squeezes — Once one pulse has been established, a new squeeze, in either direction, can be added, which will have players squeezing more often. **2. Changing length** — Squeezes can vary in pressure or in length. Longer squeezes will mean it takes longer for the squeeze to move around the circle. Players should duplicate the kind of squeeze that they received (hard, long, short, light, etc.) when they deliver the continued squeeze.

Hey Old Buddy!

Type of Game: Warm-up

Purpose: To get the players in a loud and excited mood. This game is a great character warm-up.

Group Size: The entire team

Duration: Ten minutes

Description

Have the players mingle around the room in a random pattern. Make sure that the same people are not always in the same area together. A person not mingling around (a coach or a director, etc.) picks some point to yell "Stop! Turn to the person closest to you and greet them like they are an old buddy." The players should then greet the other player like they are an old buddy. Quick introductions are the goal; one sentence each and some form of physical interaction is adequate. Ensure that the players create some form of appropriate characteristics and that the greeting is appropriate to the event. Once the players complete their introductions have them wander around the room aimlessly and have the coach stop them again to yell, "Stop! Turn to the person closest to you and greet them as your boyfriend or girlfriend who you have been away from for the summer, your arch-enemy, someone you barely remember, etc." Make sure that people are interacting with different people; the same pair of people should not be introducing themselves again and again. If there is an odd number of people, have one group of three, or have the coach play as well.

Notes

Whoever is running the game must watch how the players are responding — go with what works and cut what does not. Plus, each action takes varying amounts of time — switch when most people look finished.

Variations

1. Characteristics — Instead of relationships, use characteristics. For example, greet the person as a happy person, or as a depressed person, etc. **2. Player decides** — Instead of having a coach direct the stop and starting, have each player decide how they will greet other people. They decide this for themselves and do not declare this information before the game. Then have the players wander around the room, and every time they meet someone, they introduce themselves in the same manner that they have introduced themselves to everyone else so far. **3. Discussion** — Instead of having the players greet each other in a particular character, have them talk about something or tell each other certain things. For example, talk about the relative merits of forks versus spoons or tell each other about their favorite holiday.

Insult-o-rama

Type of Game: Warm-up

Purpose: To get the players in a loud and excited state. The game gets people's creativity flowing.

Group Size: The entire team

Duration: Five minutes, or when people start passing the line of appropriateness

Description

Have the players walk around the room and hurl the most creative insults they can at one another. The insults should not be of the Eddie Murphy stand-up variety, but of a more intelligent and innovative sort.

Notes

Make sure these insults do not become personal. You may wish to make a list of insults that would be appropriate.

Variations

1. In a field — Have players insult each other according to how someone with a certain characteristic or occupation might insult someone. Other players should respond with insults related to the same field. **2. Two groups** — Have the team divided into two groups, with each yelling insults at the other group. This can also teach proper rules of the stage, making sure everyone is heard and seen. **3. Shakespearean** — Have the players perform "Shakespearean" insults. These may take more time to come up with. **4. Gibberish** — Perform all the insults in gibberish.

Introductions

Type of Game: Warm-up
Purpose: To get things started and learn a little about everyone
Group Size: The entire team
Duration: Less than a minute each

Description

The players stand up one at a time and introduce themselves. They should give their name and some interesting "stuff" about themselves.

Notes

Introductions are important so that everyone feels a little more comfortable together. Some of the variations below can help make things more interesting.

Variations

1. Name game — The first player says their name and something else that either rhymes or starts with the same letter. For example Super Sam or Mike the Bike. The next player repeats the first player's name and gives their own. The third player lists both the first and second players' names, and so on around the circle. The first player may or may not have to repeat everyone's name. **2. Eulogy** — Players perform their introductions in the form of their own eulogy (this will tell people some of the things that the player may want to accomplish in the future). This can also become a game of its own by having players perform the eulogy of a fictional character like a superhero. **3. Tell a friend** — Players pair up and give information about each other. Then they stand up and tell the group about their partner. **4. Uniqueness** — When discussing themselves, players try and state only things about themselves that are unique to themselves (i.e., "I have an eleven-year-old brother Steven"). In the event that someone in the circle also shares the same situation, they raise their hand.

Marketing Agent

Type of Game: Warm-up
Purpose: Gets people's creativity and quick-thinking skills going
Group Size: The entire team
Duration: Five to ten minutes

Description

Have the team stand up in a line. A coach or other person yells out the name of a generic product (for example, orange juice). Starting at the end, each player must yell out the name of a "brand name" which would be suitable for the generic product, such as "A Whole Lotta Citrus." Players may not yell out the name of existing products (Minute Maid), nor can they repeat something which has been previously mentioned (A Whole Lotta Citrus) or something unrelated to the characteristic of the product (The Flying Squirrel). If a player does yell out an existing brand name, repeats a suggestion, utters something unrelated, or pauses, that player is eliminated.

Notes

If some players are eliminated very quickly and others are never eliminated, disregard the rule on elimination and have the players stay in a line, even when people err.

Variations

1. Random order — Instead of having the players speak in order, have a coach point at players randomly. **2. Ad campaign** — Instead of simply making up a product name, have the players create a slogan or a commercial/infomercial. **3. Political candidate** — Have the players create slogans for an imaginary candidate/party. **4. World's worst** — Players are given a topic and take turns doing impressions or listing titles of the world's worst versions of those things. **5 Objects** — Players are given an object and must find as many uses for it as possible. **6. Fly in my soup** — Pieces of paper are written on and placed in a bowl. Players take turns drawing from the bowl and reading: "Waiter there is a BLANK in my soup." The waiter steps forward with an appropriate punch line. **7. Top ten** — Players make up a top ten list about something.

159

Mirrors

Type of Game: Warm-up

Purpose: To increase observation skills and pay attention to the other players

Group Size: The entire team

Duration: Short

Description

Players team up in groups of two. Each team has a leader and a follower. The leader performs a variety of movements and the follower copies them (like a mirror). After awhile the players switch roles. Then eliminate the leader altogether and have both players follow each other.

Notes

The goal of this exercise is not to make the other player screw up. You are a team, and your job is to make a realistic looking mirror. Smooth movements are easier to follow than jerky ones.

Variations

1 Big group — The entire exercise can be done as a big group with one group following the movements of the other. The same progressions are used until two groups are moving in sync together with neither one leading. **2. One voice** — Instead of movement, use sound. One player is required to talk at the same time as another player. Again the job here is to work as a team to make it sound like you are talking as one. Switch back and forth as to who the leader is. Eventually you will be able to talk together with no particular leader. **3. Big voice** — By combining variations one and two you can have the entire team speaking together in one voice, quite an accomplishment for the teams that can do it. **4. The switch** — Player one begins a scene. Player two watches player one throughout the scene. The scene is later replayed with player two in player one's role. The key is to perform a detailed impression the same way the first player was performing. Another option is to continue the same scene with player two staying in the

160

role created by player one. **5. The big switch** — The team is split into two groups. Each player in group two "understudies" a player in group one. This is exactly like the switch, but on a larger scale. To make it even more difficult, do not tell players who they are studying until the switch is made.

Momentum

Type of Game: Warm-up
Purpose: To develop the ability to give and take focus
Group Size: Four to twenty
Duration: A couple of minutes

Description

One player begins by walking around the stage while the other players are frozen. The moving player has the "momentum" that they can pass on to the other players. Anytime they choose to, they can give focus to a different player through a verbal, physical, or other kind of cue, and pass on the movement. The original player freezes and the new player begins moving. Only one player should be moving at a time.

The next step is to let players take the focus. Players can begin moving at any time. When they do so the player who was moving must freeze (and give up their momentum). If two players begin moving at the same time they must mirror each other (since they are sharing their momentum).

Notes

This warm-up should teach players the idea of focus and how it must be shared. They should become aware of each other and what the other players are doing at all times. Teamwork is important if a player has become frozen in an awkward position. This warm-up game is a good lead-in to the exercises on using the focus.

Variations

1. **Two momentums** — Have two players begin, one moving faster than the other. There are now two separate and distinct momentums moving around the room. 2. **Momentum types** — Have players move in a certain way. This can be combined with the first variation to have two different types of movement moving through the room.

Pyramid Dancing

Type of Game: Warm-up

Purpose: To get the players in a fun and energetic mood. The game helps players work together in a synchronized movement.

Group Size: The entire team

Duration: A couple of minutes

Description

Have one person stand up. Two people stand behind the lead person, and three people stand behind the pair, creating a triangle shape. The person in front begins making movements, actions, or dances. The pair standing behind the lead person attempts to duplicate the actions of the lead person. The three people in the back row attempt to duplicate the movements of the pair in front of them. This game is like a physical version of the classic telephone game — much effort is put into replicating the previous instructions, with minimal success. This game is easier if the player in the lead makes slow gestures, and also avoids making rapid transitions from action to action.

Notes

Players must act in a mature way, and not make inappropriate gestures for others to copy.

Variations

1. With sound — Have the leader make sounds while making actions. People in the back must copy both the sounds and the actions.

Silly Walking

Type of Game: Warm-up

Purpose: To energize players and have them get into a fun mood

Group Size: The entire team

Duration: A couple of minutes

Description

Have the players walk around the room aimlessly. A player at random shouts out the name of a body part and then all players begin walking as if the selected body part was pulling them. Keep yelling new body parts and switching what body part the players are leading with.

Notes

This will help players walk differently than they normally do. It is a good lead up to the Character Walk Exercise.

Variations

1. Combinations — Every time a new body part is called, do not replace it, add it. In this way players walk forward with a combination of limbs leading them. **2. Bionic** — When the body part is called it becomes "bionic" and stronger and more powerful than the rest of the body. Move accordingly. **3. Pairs** — Have players walk around with another person. The pair could walk really close, in synchronization, or they could walk around keeping their bodies in contact.

Zip – Zap – Zoom

Type of Game: Warm-up

Purpose: To get reflexes up and going. The team must pay close attention to each other and must be listening intently.

Group Size: The entire team

Duration: Five minutes

Description

Have the team form a circle, either sitting or standing. One person will begin the game by turning to one of the people next to him and yelling "zip." The person who just received a "zip" then turns to the other person next to him and yells "zip." In this way a "zip" races around the circle. Now, once a player receives a "zip," he has two options: 1. Instead of just turning and zipping the person on the other side, the player who was just zipped may say "zap" at the person who had just zipped him. The person who just received this zap then turns around and says zip. This changes the direction of the zip. 2. In addition to electing to zip or zap, players who are zipped may select any person across the circle and yell "zoom." The person who was just zoomed then turns to either direction and yells "zip."

Notes

Players must push themselves to go faster. The team will get little out of the game if they proceed at a lethargic pace.

Variations

1. Two forces — Have two people start and have two "zips" moving around the circle. It is almost impossible to stay focused on both, but it is a fun way to end the game.

Blocking Game

Type of Game: Exercise (Blocking)

Purpose: To learn to recognize blocks when they happen in scenes so that they can be avoided.

Group Size: Two

Duration: Less than a minute per scene

Description

Two players go on stage. One gives an offer (for example, "let's go fishing"). The other player blocks that offer ("I don't like fishing"), and gives a new offer ("Let's do math homework instead"). Repeat this process until it grows wearisome.

Notes

If players have a problem with this, try starting with "Just say no." The easiest way to block an offer is to just say no. Then build it up to blocking without saying no.

This should be one of the first games a team plays. They need to be able to recognize blocks when they happen so that they can avoid them.

Variations

1. **One blocker** — Only one player blocks. The other player accepts the offers and tries to move the scene forward. 2. **Two realities** — Each player is given a location. They must block every attempt by the other player to make their location exist.

Yes and ...

Type of Game: Exercise (Accepting offers)
Purpose: To begin the process of accepting offers
Group Size: Two
Duration: Less than a minute per scene

Description

Two players go on stage. One makes a statement. Every statement after that must begin with "Yes and ..." Players are forced to accept the other players offer and then give something back to the other player.

Notes

There are a couple of steps in the game. The first is making sure the players actually say "Yes and ..." Many times players will fall into the "Yes and ... but ..." Do not let it happen. The next step is giving more than lip service to the acceptance of the idea. Players should say "Yes and ..." then do what is asked of them. Yes, let's go fishing; *then go fishing*! Show, don't tell!

Finally the last step is to make the acceptances of ideas follow one another. Do not just throw out one random idea after another. If one wants to go fishing then, "Yes and let's get some worms," would be a better answer than "Yes and cut my hair while we fish." This game can be played over and over again to work on the basic skills discussed in Chapter Three.

Variations

1. First to block switch — If a player blocks, have them switch places with another player. This version of the game stops working when players get good at not blocking, but it is an excellent introduction to the concept. **2. Gibberish** — Play the Yes and ... game with gibberish. **3. Mime** — Play the Yes and ... game with mime. **4. Not only/That means** — This is the over-accepting game. The idea is that every idea is accepted and then brought to the next level. "Not only is it Halloween, but the ghosts are coming out." "The ghosts are coming out, that means that we need

167

bloodhounds to track them." Every statement should involve "Not only" or "That means." **5. Fortunately/Unfortunately** — Each player is assigned a role, either "Fortunately ..." or "Unfortunately ...". Each player begins their statement with those words. Together they tell a story (with many ups and downs), *without* blocking. "The dog died," should not be followed by "Fortunately it didn't," rather by "Fortunately you were allergic to dogs."

Questions

Type of Game: Exercise (Wimping)
Purpose: To learn what wimping is and how to avoid it
Group Size: Two
Duration: Less than a minute per scene

Description
Players can only ask questions. They cannot make statements.

Notes
This game should teach players about wimping. By not making statements they delay the telling of the story.

Variations
1. First to state switch — If a player does not question, have them switch places with another player. **2. Twenty questions** — One player asks the other players questions, trying to figure out what the object is, just like a normal game of twenty questions. Only the other players do not know what the object is. (For those that have not played the game, they can only answer yes or no). After twenty questions the team should try to figure out what the object was. You will soon see that the longer it takes to define the object, the harder it is to define it.

Blind Offers

Type of Game: Exercise (Foundations — Accepting and making blind offers)
Purpose: To develop the ability to make and accept blind offers
Group Size: Two
Duration: About ten seconds per pair. Play it a few times each.

Description

Player one starts on stage and makes a physical "blind offer." This usually entails performing some random movement that they do not know the significance of (for example, banging on a box). The second player enters the stage and accepts the blind offer while "endowing" the first player with meaning (for example: "So, have the echoes told you the size of the cave?"). Player one accepts the endowment and replies to player two.

Notes

Be sure you are familiar with the idea of blind offers and endowment as discussed in Chapter Three before playing this game. The scenes should be quick and simple. The idea is to introduce the concept of making and accepting blind offers. You may wish to use this method as a start of scenes, but the first few times just run through it quickly.

The first player should not try to do something which makes sense. They should not mime doing an activity for example. If they do that the second player just ends up guessing what the first player was doing and the game becomes charades. The key to this game is that the first player has no idea so they help the second player to come up with an idea by doing a meaningless action. The end result is the beginning of a scene that neither player planned.

Variations

1. **Two lines** — Players line up in two lines with one line being the "blind offer" and the other being the acceptance. This allows the whole group to go through the game quickly. 2. **Blind acceptance** — In this version the acceptor does not see the offerer. They endow

the offerer with some meaning without knowing what their action was. The offerer then has to make sense of the combination. **3. Third wheel** — In this version one player makes a blind offer, a second player (who does not see the first player) makes a statement. This statement is treated as if the first player said it. A third player must then interact with the first player while making sense of the combined offers.

Rules of the Stage

Type of Game: Exercise (rules of the stage)

Purpose: To review and develop a team's ability to present themselves well to an audience.

Group Size: The entire team

Duration: Ten minutes

Description

There are a number of drills which will help a team improve their rules of the stage: **Voice** — Have the players say the alphabet as clearly as possible. Practice over-enunciating words. **Volume** — The coach sits at the back of the playing space, as far away from the players as possible. The players should project to the coach. **Playing down** — Place blocks behind the players that will not let them back up. Place a big X on the ground that the players must be standing on to speak. **Facing the audience** — Place stickers on the player's backs. They lose a point every time the coach can see a sticker. **Balancing the stage** — Play the creating locations games with emphasis on symmetry of the stage.

Notes

Most teams that do not have good rules of the stage, do not know what the rules are. If the team knows what is expected of them they will generally be able to do well in their presentation. The games here help to stress a point and make the players conscious of the rules.

Variations

1. Competition — If a player makes a mistake they must sub out with another player. **2. Combination** — Play these games combined with other games from this appendix. The players should always follow these rules.

The Plate Game

Type of Game: Exercise (Rules of the stage — balancing the stage)

Purpose: To make players aware of the use of space and to make players aware of their position on stage in relation to others.

Group Size: Four to eight

Duration: Five to seven minutes

Description

The team imagines the rehearsal space to be a large plate balancing on a pole. If the plate ever becomes unbalanced it topples and everyone falls to a horrible death. The only way to keep it balanced is to have players on opposite areas of the plate. For example if player one is on the extreme right hand side of the plate then in order to balance, player two has to be on the extreme left hand side. If player one moves towards the center of the plate, player two must do the same. While on the very center of the plate a player does not affect the balance. Players are free to move as often as they like as long as the plate remains balanced.

Start with two players on the plate. When the players are comfortable with the situation, add new players one at a time. The coach can also have players entering and leaving the playing area during the game. (Note that it is possible to balance with odd numbers of people, for example, with three players use a triangle formation.)

Notes

The game is more difficult and fun when players move around on the plate. You have a three-second grace period when someone moves. If you do not balance the plate in those three seconds the plate topples.

Variations

1. **Storyteller** — Have one player be the storyteller. They talk throughout the game (about nothing of importance) and are not responsible for the balance. The other players must compensate for the movements of the storyteller. 2. **Crouching** — In this variation

173

a crouching player is equal to two standing people. Therefore, if two people end up grouped together on the far-left side, one person can balance on the far-right side by crouching. **3. The jerk** — This was actually the game which originated the idea of the jerk. The team chooses a player who will intentionally try to throw the balance off. The team has to keep the plate balanced despite the efforts of the jerk.

Creating Locations

Type of Game: Exercise (Physicalization)

Purpose: To be able to work as a team to create entertaining and balanced "wheres" quickly and efficiently.

Group Size: Four to ten

Duration: Ten minutes

Description

The players stand on the stage while the coach yells out locations. When a location is called out they each become an object or animal in that location without speaking. Players should do their best not to repeat the same objects but should try to choose objects that are particular to that location (for example: a bell tower should have a bell, although it might also have benches and a balcony which could exist in other locations).

Notes

The goal of this game is to create interesting wheres very quickly. The team should attempt to balance the stage, make it symmetrical, and use different levels (see Rules of the Stage game). After they have the basics down they should be evaluated on how well they achieved these things after each location.

If players are having problems thinking of objects, remind them that if they place their body in a firm position quickly and confidently they will probably fool the audience. If they look unsure the audience will be confused even if they "know" what they are. It is best to be distinct objects, but it is better to be something (anything) than stand with your hands in your pockets.

Variations

1. Players' call — When the players get the hang of this game have them call out their own locations. **2. Mini-scenes** — Two players or so in every location take on talking roles. They then start a short scene in the location. You can even give an overall suggestion which the team is required to use in each scene (like Love, Justice, or Opposites). **3. Create a house** — In this game the players enter one at a time into the set location (for example: a house). The first player mimes using one object in the location and then leaves. The next player uses the first object and one more. This continues until everyone has entered the location.

The Environments Game

Type of Game: Exercise (Physicalizing)

Purpose: To engage imagination and all five senses when creating a where.

Group Size: Entire team

Duration: Ten to twenty minutes

Description

Team members walk around the room randomly. One at a time, players (or the coach) call out environments such as the arctic or the beach. The entire team then pretends to be in that environment by reacting non-verbally with as many senses as they can. For instance if the environment is a swamp, the team should react physically to the smell of the swamp, the dampness of the ground, etc. Once the team has explored the environment any player can call out a new environment. The team is not to become objects or animals in the environment.

Notes

There is no talking or communication in any other form in this game. The one exception is when a player calls out a new environment. When a new environment is called the players should think of temperature, footing, smells, tastes in the air, brightness of light, and any number of things that would affect their actions. The environments can be as ridiculous or far-fetched as they like (outer space, bottom of the ocean, inside the human heart) but the team still has to react to the environment with as many senses as possible.

Variations

1. **Situations** — Instead of calling out environments, players can call out situations, for instance: stuck in quicksand or baking a cake. In this variation the focus is physically acting out the situation. 2. **Not environments** — Instead of calling out environments, players can call out occupations or activities. In this variation the focus is physically becoming the character.

177

People as Objects

Type of Game: Exercise (Physicalization)

Purpose: To teach teams to listen to what is being said and physicalize foreground objects.

Group Size: Six to ten

Duration: Only a few minutes a game, but can be played a number of times

Description

Two players begin a scene while the rest of the team watches and listens in the background. The two players attempt to use objects as much as possible. When they are about to use an object a player from the back jumps up and becomes the object (note that they stay as that object for the rest of the scene). This continues until all of the background players have become objects.

Notes

The main players should not just list objects ("We need a rope. Now we need a pot. Where did I leave my box?"). They should try to create a coherent scene while using the objects.

When the main players are choosing what objects to use they should try to make them reasonable for the other players to become. A player can become a sword or a watch by keeping the majority of their body out of the action, but it is much easier for them to become a sink or a flag. It is fine to have some players playing the small objects like glasses, but variety is important. Even insubstantial things like smoke create interesting effects.

Variation

1. Rotation — Scenes can be made longer by allowing the older objects to disappear, allowing the players to become the newly created objects. With this method the game could go on indefinitely. Try to have the least important of the objects leave first.

2. Mime — A similar game can be played by not using the background players. In this game the main players just try to mime as many objects as possible. It helps to make the scene more interesting by making the players do things rather than just talking about them. **3. Make them touch** — Either version of the game can be played where you attempt to have the other player use as many objects as possible. Remember that they are not allowed to block. This can make for a high energy scene. **4. Don't let them touch** — Another variation is for a player to touch as many objects a possible while in the meantime stopping the other player from touching any. They are still not allowed to block.

Character Walk

Type of Game: Exercise (Characterization)

Purpose: To develop the ability to physicalize characters without the need for voice.

Group Size: One or two at a time, great game for a large group

Duration: About ten seconds per player. You can play it a number of times in a row.

Description

The team lines up in a row at one side of the class. Each is given a characteristic and is required to walk across the stage with that character in mind. They are not to interact with anyone, but may talk if it fits their character (i.e., their characteristic is talkative).

Notes

The point of this game is to physicalize the characters the players play. It is amazing how funny this game is. If they keep that in mind when they create their characters it will allow them to explore them in more detailed ways.

Variations

1. Criss-cross — Form two rows and have the characters cross in front of each other. The two different characters should interact in some way as they are walking by. **2. Pop-machine** — A pop-machine (or other device) is situated in the middle of the room. Without talking, the players enter the stage with their characteristic, use the pop-machine and leave. This requires that the players use their characteristics to physicalize and interact with their environment. **3. The location** — This takes the pop-machine to the next level. The players are given a location that their characters must enter, interact with, and leave. **4. Choose their own** — The players could be allowed to choose their own characteristics or attitude. This will help them develop stock characterization ability for other games. They will also discover what characters they are naturally good at playing. **5. Not characteristics** — The players could be given something other than a characteristic. It is important that they then try to link what they are given to a characteristic that they think is important. A doctor may be rich and condescending, or he could be helpful and gentle. As long as the player makes a choice, either option would be fine. Some options instead of characteristics include: occupation, animal, or hobby. **6. Random walk** — In this option the players walk randomly around the room. The coach yells out different characteristics that they take on in their walk. Notice that different players will have different interpretations.

The Character Monolog Game

Type of Game: Exercise (Characterization)

Purpose: To practice making strong, confident, and articulate characters who can exist on their own.

Group Size: One

Duration: Up to one minute per person

Description

The player is given a topic that they are required to talk about in a monolog. The player is required to create a character (other than themselves) who would be talking about the topic. The player must be able to continue talking without pausing for the entire time limit (usually one minute). Other players may not aid the player. The player may not create other characters to talk to.

Notes

Keep the topics broad the first few times you do this game. It is a better choice to have the character feel strongly one way or another about the topic. Characters who do not care are often boring. Players should not get frustrated if their mind blanks, just stay in character. An easy way to create a character with the topic is for the player to talk about an experience they had with the topic.

Voice and mannerisms are important for whatever characters are created. See Chapter Seven, Characterization, for more details on what is important.

Variations

1. **Length/Difficulty** — The length of the monolog and/or the difficulty of the topic can be changed. To force strong character choices early try time limits as short as 15 seconds. To work with players who tend to wimp, make them continue for up to five minutes. 2. **Not topics** — Instead of giving a topic, give something else and make the player come up with their own topic to talk about (this is good for use of suggestion too). Common choices include a characteristic (excellent for character game training), occupation, object, or animal. 3. **Gibberish** — To make the game

a little easier and to focus on the mannerisms and voice tone of the characters being created have the players do their monologs in gibberish.

Bus Stop

Type of Game: Exercise (Characterization)
Purpose: To utilize the basics of characterization and interaction.
Group Size: Two or more
Duration: Keep it down to about a minute per player.

Description

Each player is given (or chooses) a characteristic. The first player enters the stage and begins to wait for the bus. They show their characteristic through their actions and physicalization. There is no talking in this game

A second player enters the stage with a different characteristic. They too show their characteristic and interact (in a limited way) with the first player. Slowly the first player begins to change characteristics into the second player's characteristic. When the first player has fully changed, they get on the bus and leave. A third player enters the stage and the process continues.

Notes

This game works best if the players do not know each other's characteristics. They are forced to pay attention and pick up the mannerisms of the other players while they are in the scene. The game should not be allowed to drag on. The transitions should be fairly fast.

Finally, the characters should have a reason for changing characteristics. It is easy to just change. The challenge is finding out why they are changing.

Variations

1. **New location** — Instead of a bus stop the setting could be in an elevator, a waiting room, or other location which could have people coming and going. 2. **Don't leave** — Instead of the players leaving, they stay throughout the scene. This could get very crazy if there are a lot of players. An alternative is to have one player who never leaves, but everyone else does. **3 Talking game** — Allow the players to interact with speech. Do not do this version until players

have fully developed the ability to do it without talking. **4. The switch** — Instead of one player getting the characteristic of the other, the players switch characteristics over the course of the scene. **5. Not characteristics** — Try these games with occupations, attitudes, or physical quirks.

Opening the Box

Type of Game: Exercise (Characterization)
Purpose: Creating *Big* Characters
Group Size: Three to six
Duration: About a minute per group

Description

The players are given a reaction. They must enter the stage, open a box and react in the given way. The level of reaction depends on their position. The first player will open the box and have a mild reaction. The second player slightly more so. The second to the last player should be extreme. The last player should totally take it over the top.

Notes

Players should learn from this exercise that they should play the last character. When you are given a characteristic and are performing a scene you should be the most *blank* in the world. When players find themselves at one level of a character they should think about this exercise and bring themselves up a notch at a time until they reach the level of that last person to open the box.

Variations

1. Not a box — The same exercise can be done lots of different ways. The players may be required only to walk across the stage with their characteristic. Or they could use the pop-machine or many others. The box is a nice starting place because it is so simple. Try combining this exercise with any of the other character games in this manual.

186

Attitudes

Type of Game: Exercise (Characterization)
Purpose: To endow other players with characteristics
Group Size: Three or four
Duration: About a two-minute scene

Description

Each player is given an attitude that they must attribute to another player. For example, Bill may react with awe to whatever Lisa says and with contempt with whatever Joe says. Lisa may be saddened by whatever Bill says and excited by whatever Joe says, etc. The point is that it does not matter what the players say, it is the reaction that matters.

Notes

Start with the basics. Have two players work on stage and have one react in a certain way to whatever the other says. Then add a reaction for the other player. Finally add a third character in an experiment with more variations. Do not try to go too fast with this game — things will end up in a mess. In order for the coach to comment on the scenes and the players to improve there cannot be too much happening at one time.

Variations

1. Emotions — Try emotions instead of attitudes. **2. Tag** — One player has everyone react a certain way when he or she does things. When they touch someone else, everyone reacts that way to the new person. **3. Cocktail party** — This version works on everyone's memory too. All the players (about eight) are given different ways of reacting to each other. They all mingle in a cocktail-like setting (not a performance). They wander around talking to different people and reacting accordingly. **4. Reactions** — Players have to become used to reacting to events that happen around them. In this game all the players stand on stage. The coach yells out things that happen and all the players must react to them. In a normal scene, if something happens and the players do not react, it is the same as a block. Examples of "things that could happen" are: bit by a dog, see long-lost friend, shot in the (arm), see someone picking their nose, someone opens the door in the middle of winter, someone turns up the music. The most important thing is that the reaction is immediate and appropriate. It is more important that a choice is made than what the choice is. **5. Secrets** — Each player in the scene is given a secret, either about themselves or another player. This secret should influence the way they deal with the other characters. The secrets do not have to come out. The scene can be played as serious or comedic.

Slide Show

Type of Game: Exercise (Storytelling)
Purpose: To develop the ability to narrate a scene with actors.
Group Size: Two
Duration: A couple of minutes each

Description

Players work in pairs. One player is the storyteller and the other is the slide show. The player telling the story will flip from slide to slide as they tell the story. The other player will freeze in different positions each time the scene is "flipped."

Notes

The players must work together to tell the story. Sometimes the narrator will take the lead ("This next shot is of me climbing the mountain." Click.) and sometimes the actor will take the lead (The narrator will click and then try to explain the position the actor has taken).

The key is that both players pay attention to what the other is doing. They must work together to create the story. This is the most basic exercise to combine the two worlds of narrator and actor, and must be mastered so that stories involving the entire team can be told.

Variations

1. Entire team slide show — One narrator tells a story while the rest of the team all create tableaus that he or she explains. **2. A book** — Instead of a slide show, pages from a book could be used (These can be taken to the next level by making it a pop-up book).

Phrase at a Time

Type of Game: Exercise (Storytelling)

Purpose: To practice creating a story as a team and to get used to creating and breaking routines.

Group Size: Two or more

Duration: Ten minutes or more

Description

Players sit in a circle or line and tell a story one sentence at a time. The first player gives the first sentence. The next player continues with the next sentence, and so on. Players may not repeat what was said by the player before them.

Notes

The key to this game is making and breaking routines. The first player should set up a routine, the next player can break it and set up a new one. The third player then breaks the new routine and so on (see Storytelling, Chapter Eight, for more details on how this works). If players do not do this, they will find their stories drag on and usually make no sense.

The second step in the game involves reincorporation. Every chance the players have they should refer back to something from earlier in the story. This will give the story a sense of continuity and create an appropriate ending.

When the game is first attempted the stories should be kept simple. If too many characters or events are introduced, things will quickly become confusing and it will become difficult for the players to reincorporate all of the elements. When finished, the stories should be analyzed. Did anyone give any information that other players didn't use? Was information added that cluttered the story? Did the story drag on? Did the story have any conflict?

Variations

1. Random order — Player one says the first sentence and then points to anyone in the circle. That player gives the next sentence in the story and points to someone else somewhere else in the circle. **2. Mid-sentence** — The coach does the pointing. They can move from player to player whenever they like. The players have to be paying attention and listening so that they can be ready to pick up the story even in the middle of a word. **3. Word-at-a-time** — Players tell a story one word at a time. This is much more difficult and it is recommended that you outlaw adjectives and adverbs (which tend to operate as a form of wimping). A slight variation on this is multiple words at a time (i.e., two or three). The number could even be changed during the game.

Four Sentences

Type of Game: Exercise (Storytelling, Raising the stakes)
Purpose: To learn the important stages in telling a story.
Group Size: Three
Duration: Each game takes about two minutes.

Description

In this game each player is allowed to speak only one sentence. Each sentence acts as a stage in the telling of a story. **Player 1 — Creates an environment** through mime. This player does not talk. For example, he may start watching TV in a living room. **Player 2 — Creates a relationship** between the characters. The player says one sentence which defines the relationship. For example: "Hi dad." **Player 1 — Creates a conflict.** Using the location and relationship the first player creates conflict between the two characters. For example: "You are not watching ER tonight." **Player 2 — Raises the stakes.** The player accepts all of the previous elements created and makes things worse. This sentence should advance the story and heat up the conflict. For example "Why don't you get a job instead of watching TV all the time?" **Player 3 — Resolves the story.** While player one and two keep quiet the third player enters and speaks their sentence. This sentence should accept everything which came before it. The statement should end the scene while still incorporating the things which came earlier. For example: "Honey, the plant is hiring, take a look at the news on channel four."

Notes

The players should be walked through the game the first time. It may take a little while for them to get used to it. It is essential that they keep their statements down to one sentence each. This is an exercise and not a performance.

Variations

1. Off-stage dialog — To avoid the problem of players speaking too much, try having off-stage players do voice-overs for the dialog. **2. Gibberish** — For a slightly easier game try doing the scene in gibberish. It will still teach the essential elements of a story.

Controlling Their Actions

Type of Game: Exercise (Moving the scene forward)
Purpose: To learn to make and accept offers.
Group Size: Two
Duration: About a two minute scene

Description

Two players describe each other's movements. Every time player one finishes their dialog, player two adds their physical action. For example:

A: Would you like to go to tea?

B: *He said as he pulled out a gun.*

B: I would love to.

A: *She said as she tore off her outer clothes to reveal that she was Wonder Woman.*

A: Oh my I am so sorry.

B: *He said, cowering in fear.*

Etc.

Notes

Players should attempt to move the story with every offer that they make. They should not force the story in a particular direction by blocking or waffling on the other person's ideas. The actions do not necessarily have to fit with the dialog (although it must make sense in the end).

Variations

1. Moving bodies — Stagehands move the bodies of the acting players. Either each player has their own "marionette" or one stagehand may have to control more than one player. The acting players should move easily when the stagehands direct them. Otherwise they do not move at all. **2. Moving bodies with momentum —** The same idea as the first variation, only now the actors will continue moving after the puppeteer leaves. If the stagehands start an arm in one direction, it will continue in that direction until they (or another stagehand) stop it.

193

Interconnections

Type of Game: Exercise (Storytelling - Reincorporating)
Purpose: To be able to build on what has come before.
Group Size: Five to twelve
Duration: About fifteen to twenty minutes

Description

The first player begins by describing their character who lives in a small town. They should make some mention of family, occupation, etc. The next player continues by describing their character. They should make at lest one connection to the first character (i.e., I get my hair cut at his barbershop). The third player describes their character and makes separate connections to each of the first two characters. This process continues until everyone has participated and every character has a distinct connection to every other character.

A scene is played that takes place in the small town and the characters interact in appropriate ways.

Notes

This exercise results in very detailed interconnection. The resulting scenes can go on for a long time exploring these connections. The point of this exercise is to show how incredibly intricate scenes can be created in a short amount of time. It is easy to take these same ideas and do the scene without the original build-up.

Variations

1. Three monologs — Three players are on stage. They are given an event (example: meteor hitting the Earth, stepping on a spider, ice cream cone melting, etc.). They tell the story of that event in three intertwined monologs from different points of view. The first character should be the "main character," the second has a quite different point of view, and the third is something outlandish. For example, the first might be the person stepping on the spider, the second person the spider, and the third the shoe. Make sure that the players do not repeat each other (delaying), they want to continue the story from where the other person left off, but from a new point of view. The story should jump from player to player and not proceed in the same order every time.

Story Expansion

Type of Game: Exercise (Storytelling)
Purpose: Develop the ability to tell a coherent story.
Group Size: Two to ten
Duration: Ten minutes or so

Description

The first player makes a statement in the present tense. The second player then says "What you're saying is that ... (the statement) ... so I'll ... (new statement)." This continues through the entire team. For example:

A: I am going for a walk.

B: *What you're saying is* I am going for a walk *so I'll* wear my Walkman.

C: *What you're saying is* I am wearing my Walkman *so I'll* play loud music.

D: *What you're saying is* I am playing loud music *so I'll* dance to the beat.

Etc.

Notes

This game is really a variation of phrase at a time in a new form. It will teach teams to tell a coherent story so that things make sense. Make sure that each statement relates to the statement before it (and not one of the statements from earlier on in the story).

The variation below is another game which will help players develop their storytelling abilities.

Variations

1. Unrelated questions — One player tells a story. After each statement the coach (or another player) asks an unrelated question which continues the story. For example:

I went into a house. *What was in the house?*
There was a lot of furniture in the house. *What did your mother say?*
My mom was mad I had run off. *Why was the girl in the house?*
I had planned to meet my girlfriend there. *Why was she crying?*

The questioner should try to be specific about some things, but general about others. They do not want to do all the work for the player, but they also do not want them to struggle to reincorporate the facts given to them.

The Object

Type of Game: Exercise (Use of suggestion)

Purpose: To develop the ability to use a suggestion the way it was meant to be used.

Group Size: One or Two

Duration: Less than a minute each

Description

The player is given the suggestion of an object. They mime killing themselves using the object.

Notes

The key in this scene is to have the players use the object in a way that only that object could be used. If given a fly swatter they should not hit themselves with it, they could do that with any object. They must find what makes the object unique and use those elements. A fly swatter is used to kill flies, so perhaps they could use a teleportation booth (as in *The Fly*) to mold their DNA with that of a fly and then start swatting themselves. Remember that if they could kill themselves in the way they do with a different unrelated object, then they have not done their job of using their suggestion.

Variations

1. Escape from the island — Teams of two players must escape from a desert island with only the object. Make sure it is used in a way that only the object can be used. **2. Get the job** — Players must use their skill with the object in an occupational setting. This is combining two suggestions so make sure the object is used in a way to do something that makes the occupation distinctive. **3. Solve the problem** — More generally, give the player a problem and an object. They must use the object to solve the problem. **4. The hunter** — The hunter walks on stage and talks to himself about hunting *blank*. A second player comes on as the *blank* and kills the hunter in a way related to the suggestion. He becomes the new hunter until everyone has had a turn.

Combining Suggestions

Type of Game: Exercise (Use of suggestion)

Purpose: To be able to combine unrelated suggestions into a coherent scene.

Group Size: Two to ten

Duration: About a three-minute scene

Description

The players are given two unrelated suggestions. They are required to create a scene that combines both of these suggestions at the same time.

Notes

The key to this scene is to combine the suggestions. It is easy to use the suggestions one after another (which is often what is done when teams ask for more than one suggestion), the trick is to combine them in a unique way. Some examples of suggestions that can be given include:

- Two locations
- Two animals
- A choice and a moral
- A sport and an object

Any of the above choices can be combined (an animal and a moral). Check out the list of ask-fors (beginning on page 250) for more options.

Variations

1. Verb/noun game — Players are given a verb and a noun and must tell the story of "The verbing of the noun." **2. Fairy tales** — The players are given a fairy tale which is changed in some way (i.e., the introduction of a new character).

199

Changing the Focus

Type of Game: Exercise (rules of the stage/teamwork)

Purpose: A more advanced exercise which teaches teams to share the focus on stage.

Group Size: Four

Duration: About twenty minutes to run through the variations

Description

Part 1 — Two pairs of players go on-stage. Both groups are to have a conversation about something minor (favorite color or favorite TV show). The audience watches and points to the group that they are watching. The player's job is to get as many people watching them as possible (get the focus). **Part 2** — Now have the players attempt to send the focus back and forth. The group which does not have the focus should be paying attention to when the first group is trying to send the focus. The group with the focus should be paying attention to when the second group is trying to take the focus.

Notes

The key to the first exercise is to be loud, excited, and move around a lot. The players should learn what it takes to get the audiences' attention. The second part teaches them how to avoid their attention. It should also help them pay attention and listen to the rest of the team. It is important that players not talk over each other and this game should teach that.

Variations

1. Table talk — A more advanced version of this game has up to three sets of players sitting at tables. Each group should be having a conversation and should come in and out of focus. To make it more interesting have all the stories interconnect in some way (although the different tables should not know each other or interact in any way). **2. Cocktail party** — An even more advanced version of this game has all of the players wandering around in a cocktail party. They all have different stories to tell to each other. The focus must constantly shift through the party. **3. Telephone**

criss-cross — The players are having phone conversations. The focus changes from one conversation to the next. All of the changes should take place on specific words ("I just got a new car ..." "*Car! Car!* I said, but it would not move ..."). Try to use different volumes, tones, and speeds of speech.

Sit-Stand-Lie Down

Type of Game: Exercise (Rules of the stage - levels)

Purpose: To understand the use of levels while working together as a team.

Group Size: Four

Duration: About a two-minute scene

Description

There are four positions in this game: sitting, standing, lying down, and kneeling (a fifth position of "squatting" could be added if an extra one is needed). Four players participate in this scene and all of the positions must be represented at all times. So, if the sitting player stands up, the standing player is forced to sit down.

Notes

This game works two different skills. Primarily it teaches the team about the idea of using different levels in a scene. This aspect should be stressed and the team should understand why levels make a scene more interesting to watch.

The second skill this game teaches is the ability to watch and pay attention to the other players on stage. If any of the players move, the others must be ready to change their positions quickly and efficiently. Players should always watch what the others are doing.

Variations

1. **More players** — If more players are desired, either extra positions could be added (like crouching), or some positions may be given to multiple players.

Options

Type of Game: Exercise (Use of Suggestion)

Purpose: To help players learn to incorporate suggestions. The game also forces players to prepare themselves for sudden twists in the scene.

Group Size: The entire team

Duration: About three-minute scenes

Description

The team begins the scene. At any point in the scene, a coach or outside player yells "freeze." The team must immediately freeze in whatever position they are in. At this point the coach yells out a suggestion for the scene to take (examples of suggestions for this game include: problems, new characteristics, locations, styles, etc.) Once the coach has yelled the suggestion, the coach yells "un-freeze," at which point the team unfreezes and continues with the scene. The team must incorporate the new suggestion as fast as possible, and they also must make a solid attempt to justify and rationalize the sudden twist in the scene.

Notes

The team should incorporate the new suggestions into the scene immediately and explore the new suggestions. They should not simply mention the new suggestions and continue with their original plan.

Suggestions may be related in some way to the scene, or they may be entirely irrelevant.

Variations

1. **Paper** — Write down a number of suggestions on scraps of paper. Scatter them around the floor of the playing surface. Have the team perform a scene and every fifteen seconds or so, pick up a piece of paper and incorporate the paper's idea into the scene. Instead of a one word suggestion, write down full sentences for the team to use as dialog, or write physical actions that the team must demonstrate. 2. **Should have said** — After a player has said

something, either through dialog or narration, the coach yells out, "Should have said," at which point the person who had just spoken must backtrack and say something else.

For example: "I walked into the house"
　　　　　"Should have said" ... "saloon"
　　　　　"Should have said" ... "space station"

3. Choose your own adventure — Any time a player has a choice it is made by someone outside the action (i.e., coach, audience, etc.) **4. What if?** — The scene is played one way, then is done again under a different choice which was made early in the scene.

Categories

Type of Game: Exercise (Use of suggestion)

Purpose: To develop the ability to use a suggestion in a number of original ways.

Group Size: The entire team

Duration: Two minute scenes

Description

Before starting a scene, every member on the team is given a "category of knowledge." The team then performs a standard improvised scenario. In the scene, each player must make as many references, puns, and analogies as possible, all in the context of the scene. For example, if Reggie's special field was "airplanes," he might describe his day as "sunny, with a twenty-five kilometer per hour wind from the northeast." He might describe his marriage as "smooth sailing," etc.

Notes: Players should aim for variety in the kind of comments they make. Comments should not be forced, but rather natural observations in the context of the scene.

This is an incredible game to help players incorporate the suggestion into scenes without simply repeating the name of the suggestion over and over.

Variations

1. Limited knowledge — To increase the difficulty of the game, the players can be given categories in areas in which they have limited knowledge. For example, if Fred is a football quarterback, instead of being given "football," he could be given "painting." This forces players to deal with suggestions that they are not very familiar with.

The Hot Dog Stand

Type of Game: Training game (fundamentals — characterization and teamwork)

Purpose: To exercise feeding a characteristic and to help teams find as many different ways to feed a character.

Group Size: Two or more

Duration: About thirty seconds per player

Description

A player is chosen to act as the "character." The character runs a hot dog stand. They are given a characteristic but are cautioned not to show it unless they are "fed" by another player. The other players take turns entering the scene and feeding the vendor. Each player should attempt to feed the characteristic in a different way.

Notes

The first words players say when they enter the scene should be the character feed. It is easy to fall into the trap of entering and saying "Hi" or "I would like a hot dog." That could be said for any characteristic, instead they should find something distinct that will show the characteristic in a specific way. The same feed should not be used more than once.

Players have two options when they enter to feed. They could interact with the character (i.e., if the characteristic is angry they could bump into him giving him a reason to be angry) or they could just enter and say something to the "fourth wall" which shows the characteristic without requiring the main character to do anything ("Why is the old hot dog vendor just lying there dead?"). See Feeding in Chapter Ten, Teamwork, for more information.

Variations

1. Character tag — The players switch playing the main character each time. For example, Joe gets fed and then leaves. Francis becomes the vendor with the characteristic and Mark enters and feeds her. Francis is replaced with Mark, and so on. For this game the reason for leaving should be related to the characteristic.

2. Reversed vendor — In this version the hot dog vendor does not have a characteristic. Instead everyone who enters the scene does and the vendor is expected to feed each of them in turn. **3. Feeding characters** — The players who are entering and feeding are given characteristics too. They have to feed the vendor in a way which relates to their own characteristic as well as theirs. Much harder. **4. Different location** — The game is set at some other location instead of a hot dog stand. It could be another place of work or even something simple like a park bench. The players attempt to use feeds which combine the location and the characteristic.

Raising the Stakes

Type of Game: Exercise (Teamwork)

Purpose: To learn to enter from the background of a scene and raise the stakes.

Group Size: Three to twelve

Duration: A couple of minutes

Description

One player is given an objective or goal they must accomplish (for example, studying for a test or asking someone out). They are prevented from achieving their goal by an obstacle (A friend who does not want to study or the girl's friends who will not leave them alone). While they are trying to achieve their goal, players in the background should come up one at a time and raise the stakes of the scene. They do this by making it more important that the player achieve their goal. For example, in the studying example they could enter and say "Wow, that test coming up is going to be really hard," or "I hear the average you need for college is going to get higher."

They can also raise the stakes by helping out the obstacle, "The party of the year is going to be starting in TEN MINUTES!" Anything that makes it harder for the main player or makes what they are trying to do more important are excellent choices for raising the stakes.

Notes

The players that raise the stakes should come in, raise the stakes and get out. They should not be in the scene very long, just enough time to make things worse for the main player and leave.

This is a very important game and teams should practice it until they are quite good at it. It shows teamwork and teaches the necessary skills to tell a story (or perform a scenario) well. See Raising the stakes in Chapter Ten, Teamwork, for more information.

Variations

1. **Different problems** — The game can be played again and again by choosing new goals and new obstacles. 2. **Scenario** — Give the

208

team a scenario and have them figure out what the goal and obstacles should be on their own.

Endowment Game

Type of Game: Exercise (Listening, Teamwork)

Purpose: To pay attention to the other players and perform a coherent scene.

Group Size: Two to ten

Duration: About a two-minute scene

Description

One player leaves the room (this is also known as "blind games" since the player is blind as to what is going to happen). The other players are then given the suggestion as to **who** the missing player is, **where** the scene takes place, **what** the player did (or what has just happened or **why** the player did it), or some other component. The player then comes back in and must play the scene while trying to figure out what is going on. There are many examples of scenes like this which are played often:

1. Superhero/famous person — The player is someone famous or "superfamous."

2. Criminal/Boris/terrorist — The player is being interrogated for a crime (but they do not know what the crime is).

3. Expert/occupation — Player is an expert on something, but they do not know what.

4. Location — Player walks into a location physicalized by the rest of the team. They begin using the people as the objects that they think they are.

5. Storytelling charades — See Telephone Charades Variation game.

Notes

These game are not charades. The other players act as they would if the player knew what they were (give hints, but do not give it away). The main player struggles to figure out what they are or what they should know. This game can be played in front of an

210

audience who often finds the process very amusing.

Variations

1. Party host — The host of a party (or bartender or travel agent or taxi driver or ... you get the idea) has a number of guests arrive. The host should know who each of the guests are, but does not. The host must figure out who the guests are without letting them know he has no idea of their identities.

Mixed-up Huddle

Type of Game: Exercise (The Huddle, Teamwork)

Purpose: To pay attention to the other players and perform a coherent scene.

Group Size: Four to ten

Duration: About a four-minute scene

Description

The coach creates two scenarios. Two players (who will be the main players in the scene) are given one of the scenarios, the rest of the team is given the other scenario. The scenario given to the rest of the team is the scenario that is the "right one." The scene is played and it is up to the background players to get the scene back on track. It is up to the main players to figure out what is going on and follow the leads that the background players bring in.

Notes

This exercise is of great use when a team has had difficulty listening in the huddle. Often times players will start a scene and already have forgotten what their suggestion was. At these times it is up to the players who remember the suggestion to go into the scene and get things back on track. The scene will not be fun to watch, but it teaches an important skill — troubleshooting.

Variations

1. Messed-up player — In this version one of the main players gets the wrong suggestion and one gets the right suggestion. It is up to them to figure out who heard it right by listening to the feeds by the background characters.

Chant

Type of Game: Exercise (Teamwork)
Purpose: To develop the voice while working as a team.
Group Size: Three
Duration: A minute

Description

Each player is given a statement from a different category (or is allowed to pick their own). Categories may include: Shakespeare, the Bible, advertising slogans, famous quotes, song lyrics, etc. The players chant their lines one after another. After they have all chanted their lines they begin to intermix their lines over each other. The idea is to create a pleasing sound, not a mess.

Notes

This game is not included in the singing/rhyming section because it should not be considered an advanced skill. Most teams should be able to perform this exercise. The goal is not to create fabulous singers, but to teach players how to share focus. For this game to work well the players must change tempos and beats in such a way that they compliment and not overpower each other.

Variations

1. **Storytelling** — A variation of the "Phrase at a Time" game. One player chants a line and continues chanting that line. The next player adds the next line and continues chanting it. The third player adds in their line (so now all three players are chanting together). After the third player has chanted their line twice, the first player drops their line and adds the fourth line to the story. This continues so that all three players are chanting all the time and the story is moving forward.

Telephone Charades

Type of Game: Exercise (Teamwork)

Purpose: To pay attention to other players and get your point across to them.

Group Size: Two to ten

Duration: Ten minutes

Description

There are a number of ways to do this, but here is one. The first player is given a location, an object, and an occupation. They mime the occupation using the object within the location for a second player. When the second player thinks they have figured out what is going on they say so. The second player repeats the process to the third player. This continues down the line until everyone has had a turn. The last player tells the first player what the scenario was, and everyone laughs when it's not quite right.

Notes

Obviously this is a combination of charades and the telephone game (see the variations below if you are unfamiliar with these games). This game teaches both elements at the same time. Players will learn to watch and pay attention to each other. They will also develop skills at physicalizing and making themselves understood.

HINT: Keep each of the elements presented separate and distinct. It makes it easier to decipher.

Variations

1. Charades — Players are given suggestions that they must act out so the other players can guess what they are. **2. Storytelling charades** — One player does not know any of the suggestions. They must tell the story that the other players are acting out. **3. Telephone** — A player whispers something to the player next to them (or reads a complicated statement). This message is passed from player to player around the circle until the last player tells the first player what they thought the message was. This is really just a listening game.

Playing It Real

Type of Game: Exercise (Playing a genuine character)

Purpose: Learning how to play a real and genuine character on stage.

Group Size: Pairs to larger group

Duration: Twenty minutes

Description

This exercise has four steps:

1. Talk to someone — The players split up into pairs and talk about themselves in a natural way about something that they know about. They should keep it simple and not try to be funny.

2. With an audience — A pair of players is placed in front of the rest of the group. One player talks to the other exactly as they were before, only now with people listening.

3. To the audience — The player who they were talking to leaves the stage. The player is left alone and just talks to the audience as if they were their old partner.

4. About something else — The player keeps the same tone and attitude and begins speaking about something they do not know a lot about (given by the coach). They must talk in exactly the same manner as they were before.

Notes

This game is much harder than it sounds. The goal is to have players who can play real people on stage (see Chapter Twenty, Reality-Based Structures, for more detail). This exercise is of great benefit to those who wish to use their improvisation skills in conventional theatre. It will also help players who have trouble relaxing on stage.

Variations

1. More so — Eventually teams who are comfortable with each other can take this exercise to a higher level by talking about things that are very important to them (or moving, or sad, or hard to talk about). Go through the same steps above with the new story, then take the same intensity and apply it to something unrelated. Good luck.

215

Intensities

Type of Game: Exercise (Intensity)

Purpose: To be able to create variety in a scene by changing the levels of intensity.

Group Size: Two to ten

Duration: About a four-minute scene

Description

The team performs a scenario given to them by the coach. During the scenario the coach yells out different levels of intensity. The team continues the scene at the new level given. They should have reasons for changing from one level to the next. The changes should not be arbitrary. For example, in a scene about a boy and a girl the coach yells out "four."

Girl: I think I am going to break up with you.

Boy: I see.

Coach: Ten.

Girl: HOW CAN YOU SAY THAT I ...

Coach: One.

Girl: (silence)

Boy: (silence)

Coach: Seven.

Boy: Well, what do you want me to say?

And so on ...

Notes

Changing intensities adds a lot of variety to scenes. Changing arbitrarily just causes confusion. The team should understand that this exercise is to help explore their range and normal scenes should not be done like this. Players should learn from this exercise the possible levels of intensity available to them, and when they are effective. Intensity does not just mean volume. A scene does not have to be loud to be intense. Sometimes quiet scenes are the most intense of all. Try playing scenes where the volume must stay the same while the intensity level changes. Note that this exercise is really just a variation of the Style Rollercoaster game, but because it teaches different skills, it has been included as its own game.

Variations

1. Visually — The changing intensities can be done visually with the coach holding their hand at different levels. The higher the hand the higher the intensity. This insures that the players are always watching and paying attention during the scene. **2. Silence** — Try playing games in which silences are used. These silences can be chosen by the players or directed by the coach.

The Jerk

Type of Game: Exercise (Teamwork)
Purpose: To be able to cope when things do not go as planned.
Group Size: Four to ten
Duration: Not very long

Description

This exercise can be done with any game. Play the game as normal except with one "jerk." The jerk player comes into the scene and tries to ruin it. The other players must cope with the actions of the jerk and make the scene make sense.

Notes

One would hope that no player would ever intentionally try to ruin a scene (especially during a performance), but people make mistakes. This exercise will teach teams what to do if things do not go as they planned. This exercise works especially well for the games that may be used in a performance. If they can survive the jerk, then they can handle just about anything.

As the jerk, the player should try to ruin things, but make himself look good. It's easy to walk into a scene and just start screaming so no one can hear what is being said, but this is not what the jerk is about. The jerk should try to be subtle and just send things off in the wrong direction. In a narrated scene the jerk should do things the narrator does not expect. In all scenes the jerk should block and wimp whenever it is not appropriate.

Variations

1. Improv nightmare — In this version only one player is not the jerk. That player must try to keep the scene going while everyone else tries to destroy it. Not for beginning players.

Freeze Game

Type of Game: Practice Game (Short spontaneous scenes)
Purpose: To develop spontaneity and teamwork.
Group Size: Four or more
Duration: As long as you like

Description

Players form a circle. Two players start in the center of the circle. Two other players mold the first two players in any position. The first two players start a scene based on the positions they are in. Players in the scene must freeze immediately when a player in the circle claps. After a player claps, he/she may tap a "frozen" player and take on that player's position and then start a new scene based on their positions. The player who was tapped joins the circle.

Notes

Try to avoid just talking. The scene needs action in order for the players to get into interesting positions for other people to use for the scene. Nobody will be able to clap in if there are always two people standing and talking. The player must freeze immediately when they hear the clap. The newest player in always starts the scene.

Variations

1. **Multiple players** — Three or four players are in the circle instead of just two. 2. **Theme game** — The game is given a theme that all the scenes have to relate to. This can be vague like "Hope" or "Needs" or specific like Socks, Weathermen, or Fairy tales. 3. **Forced clapping** — Sometimes scenes drag on too long and players do not clap in when they should. This variation has the coach, or someone designated by the coach, doing the clapping and sending in the players. 4. **Increasing players** — Whenever a player claps into a scene no one else leaves. This means that the game will start with one player, then go to two, then three, then four, etc. The game can be done in reverse with the coach clapping out players in the order they entered. 5. **Continuing characters** —

Each player plays the same character every time they enter a scene. **6. Related event** — Players are given an event and they do various scenes at different points in time related to the event, but do not do the actual event itself.

Typewriter Game

Type of Game: Practice Game (Storytelling)
Purpose: To introduce the idea of storytelling as a team.
Group Size: Four to ten
Duration: First attempts should consist of two-minute stories.

Description

This is the basic storytelling game. One player sits and types at an imaginary typewriter. They say aloud everything they are typing. The rest of the players mime the scenes the author describes. When teams are comfortable with the basics some of the actors can add dialog, for example:

Author: The man pulled out a gun. He said to the lady ...

Actor #1: Give me your money.

Author: The lady replied ...

Actor #2: Never! I will never stop my fight against tyranny!

And so on ...

Notes

This is as basic a game as possible for telling a story. It is not to say it is easy or boring. Doing this scene well can be quite difficult, and when done well it can be a very entertaining scene. Teams should practice this game until they get the hang of it. The actors should obtain more and more anonymity every time the game is played. Eventually it should not be apparent who is leading the scenes, the players or the narrator.

Most storytelling games with a narrator are just variations on this simple game. Be familiar with it and any other storytelling game will be much easier.

Some "gimmicks" that are often used in this game include:

* **White out** — The author decides that something did not work, so goes back and changes it.

221

- **Dramatic pause** — At some exciting part of the story the author runs out of paper and has to pause to get some new sheets.
- **Interaction** — The characters in the story decide they do not like how the author is writing and "rebel."

Use the gimmicks with caution. You do no want the structure to start overshadowing the suggestion.

Variations

1. **Everything ...** — Any game with a narrator is a variation of this basic game. Look through the list of games and see what similarities you can find.

Style Rollercoaster

Type of Game: Practice Game ("How" events)
Purpose: To explore a wide variety of styles.
Group Size: Three to eight
Duration: About four minutes, but can be much longer.

Description

The players receive a story title or well-known story (i.e., a fairy tale) from the coach or audience. They begin by telling the story. Through the scene the coach calls out styles (see the Lists Appendix). When a style is called out, the story continues but changes to fit the new style. For example, if they were telling the story of *Little Red Riding Hood*, it might begin with Little Red Riding Hood leaving for Grandma's house. When the coach yells "western" the team may start humming "western music" and the girl is approached by a gun wielding wolf who says this town isn't big enough for the two of them. When the coach calls "children's show" a narrator may explain why it is bad to talk to strangers.

Notes

It is important not to lose track of the story. The simpler it is the easier it will be to show the changing styles. It is a great game to try out a large number of styles very quickly to see if your team is naturally talented at any particular one. If they find one they are good at they may want to consider spending some time making a structure for it (see Part Three, Structuring).

This game can also be done in performance either with a set list of the styles to be used or with the genres gathered from the audience.

Variations

1. **Not styles** — The game can be done with different things instead of styles. Characteristics, occupations, emotions, adjectives, even university majors have been done in the past.
2. **Line up** — In this variation the team tells the story but does not act it out. Each player is given a style or genre and when it is their

223

turn to speak they continue the story in their style. This is sort of a cross between this game and the Phrase at a Time game. **3. Combinations** — Try having two lists so that scenes must be combinations of elements from both (for example, a happy western or plumber opera). **4. Quadrants** — The stage is divided up into sections. Each part of the stage has its own "style." When players are in that part of the stage they must play that style.

Scene Three Ways

Type of Game: Practice Game (Genre exploration)

Purpose: To increase skill of "doing things" while exploring a variety of styles.

Group Size: Three to ten

Duration: About six or seven minutes per set

Description

The team acquires a few ask-fors and performs a "straight" scene that can be funny, but is not required to be. After the scene is done they perform the same scene again with a different genre. The same things should happen (the what) with the same characters (the who), but how things happen should change (the how). This is generally done for two different genres (hence Scene Three Ways).

Notes

The team should concentrate on keeping the **what** the same. If a player drops something in the first scene they should drop it in the next two scenes as well. The action (and dialog) in the scenes should be kept as unchanged as possible, just **how** things are happening should change.

Apart from being a good way to explore styles, teams will quickly discover how important it is to do things. If the first scene was just people standing around and talking then it will be hard to put in elements from the different styles in the later scenes. If the team knows what styles they will be doing before they start their first scene, some elements from those styles may filter in. Try to keep the first scene as neutral as possible and the later scenes will have more of an effect.

Variations

1. More than three — In order to try out more styles quickly a team can do scene four ways or scene ten ways. They just keep playing the same scene over and over with different styles. **2. Not styles —** the scenes can be re-done in different ways without resorting to styles. For example, scenes can be done with different characteristics or occupations. **3. Points of view** — This is a more specialized version of number two. Scenes are replayed from a different character's point of view. Things may change even more than the other formats (different people may hear different things when something is said). This format can be used when eyewitnesses describe what happened at the scene of a crime or when two people complain how the other ruined the date.

Set Phrases

Type of Game: Practice Game (Reincorporation)
Purpose: Utilize the suggestions and not pre-plan scenes.
Group Size: Three to ten
Duration: About a four-minute scene

Description

The audience (or coach or other players) write down a statement on cue cards (try no questions). For example a card might say "I have learned how to fly," or "My mother is missing." Anything will do. The cards are divided up by the players and at various points in the scene the players will read their dialog from these cards.

Notes

It is important that players use the elements that are brought out when they read from their card. It is easy to just say things, get a laugh and then ignore them. The key to this game is to combine the elements from each one of the statements (i.e., "Let's fly around then and see if we can find my mother"). There is a fine balance between using the cards too much and not using them enough. Try it out and find out where the ideal operation level is for your team.

Variations

1. Actor's nightmare — One player reads all of their lines from a play (either picked by the audience or supplied by the coach). The other player tries to rationalize why these things are being said. Note that it is wimping just to fall back on calling the other player crazy. **2. First line/last line** — In this scene the players are only given the first and last line of dialog. It is up to the players to get the scene from one place to the next. As an added challenge only some of the players may know what those lines are, so the rest of the team will be required to follow their lead. **3. On the ground** — This is a minor variation. Place all of the cards on the ground. The players then pick a card off the ground when they are going to speak.

Alphabet Game

Type of Game: Practice Game (Think before you speak)
Purpose: Make players share the stage with others.
Group Size: Two to five
Duration: A couple of minutes per pair

Description

This is a normal scene, but every time a player speaks they must begin their statement with the next letter of the alphabet. For example:

"**A**nother nice day."

"**B**etter believe it."

"**C**an you pass me the water?"

"**D**on't you think you can get it yourself?"

And so on ...

Notes

The team must remember to continue to use whatever suggestion was given. This is an easy game to get knocked off track for no reason. The main purpose of this game (other than being funny when players get good at it) is to put the very strong players on an even footing with newer players. They are both forced to work through this scene slowly and get better at it together. The same principle holds with the variations below.

Variations

1. Five letter word — The players are given a five letter word. Instead of working through the alphabet players work their way through the word over and over again until the scene is done.
2. Different letters — Each player is given a different letter with which they must begin all of their sentences. **3. Word count** — Instead of using the alphabet, count the number of words in each phrase. The first statement should be one word, the second two words, the third three words, etc. Upon reaching ten (or some other pre-picked number) either count back down, or just start at one

again (this could also be done with syllables instead of words). **4. Two plus three** — By combining options two and three you can give each player a number and all of the statements they speak must contain that many words. **5. Speaking in turn** — Players must speak in a certain order. **6. Alliteration** — Players are given one letter and they must incorporate that letter as many times as possible. **7. No "S"** — Players perform a scene in which they never use the letter "S" (or another pre-chosen letter) in any part of the words they are using. This does not mean dropping the "S" from words. Rather, words with "S" should be avoided altogether.

Literary Effects

Type of Game: Practice Game (Storytelling, literary elements)

Purpose: To discover some of the literary techniques that can be used in a scene.

Group Size: Three to ten

Duration: About a four-minute scene

Description

The players perform a scene in which they use one or more literary effects throughout the scene. Some effects that work well are: **1. Flashbacks** — The characters in the scene are constantly having flashbacks to some earlier time. Any time a player "thinks back" the team acts out that flashback scenario. **2. Dreams** — The characters are considering the future or what-if-scenarios. **3. Asides** — The players are continually making asides to the audience on what they are thinking. These asides take place during normal conversations, and the other players cannot hear them. **4. Soliloquies** — Taking asides further, players will break into long monologs whenever they have to make a decision or think about something. Again the other players cannot hear what is happening. **5. Memories** — Scenes are interrupted by important people from the character's past who add insight into current events. **6. Foreshadowing** — Things happen which foreshadow things that happen later. It is essential that the later things eventually happen. **7. Metaphors** — The team is required to speak in metaphors as much as possible. **8. Voice-overs** — Off-stage players perform voice-overs for the players on stage.

Notes

By having the players concentrate on one of the literary elements at a time, they can begin to understand its uses. Soon they will be able to implement these skills into all of their scenes (when they are useful). After experimenting with each one of the effects, try making scenes which use two of the elements, then three, then four until the team uses them without forcing them.

Variations

1. By the player — Each player is given one of the elements that they will use continually throughout the scene.

The Rehearsal

Type of Game: Practice Game (Narrator variation)
Purpose: Work with a narrator in a different setting.
Group Size: Three to ten
Duration: About a four-minute scene

Description

The scene is actually a rehearsal and not a real scene. At different points during the scene the action is interrupted by a director who changes the focus, or has the players do things again, only differently.

Notes

This game is really a combination of the Style Rollercoaster and Video Editing games. The director can have the players do things different ways (i.e., with different characteristics or styles) or do many of the things they can do with video editing (i.e., repeat things, faster or slower, rotate the action, etc).

Variations

1. **Differing actors** — The "actors" can be portrayed very differently than the characters they are playing in the scene. For example the tender princess may be played by a mean actress who gets upset every time the director interrupts. This effect can also be achieved by assigning the characters and actors different characteristics. 2. **... Within a play ...** — A third level of action can be added (i.e., directed scene is itself a scene and the director is really an actor). 3. **Other variations** — Look at Video Editing and Style Rollercoaster games for more variations which can be used with this scene.

Video Editing

Type of Game: Practice Game (Teamwork, Movement Skills)

Purpose: To utilize storytelling skills in a specialized setting.

Group Size: Three to ten

Duration: About a four-minute scene. You can spend quite a while flagging this game.

Description

The basic premise of this game is that the narrator is in a video editing room. The narrator does not tell the story (that is left to the players on stage), instead he or she will use the devices in the video editing room to change the action. They have a number of abilities at their disposal: **1. Change speed** — They can fast forward or slow down the scene. **2. Change direction** — They can reverse the action (and can do it more than once at any point). **3. Change camera angle** — They can show top-down shots, bottom-up shots, reverse shots, and close-ups. **4. Sound** — they can increase and decrease the volume or mute the sound and even do voice-overs. **5. Pause** — They can stop the action altogether. **6. Special effects** — They can add special effects to the scene like monsters, explosions, or laser beams. **7. The pen** — They can draw on the scene to point something out to the audience.

Notes

This game is very gimmicky. If you play it more than a few times you will find all of the jokes coming from the same places. The first couple of times it is played it can be a lot of fun. For the game to work the players need to be on the ball and continually setting each other up. Scenes with lots of very physical action are funnier in reverse than scenes with talking heads. The team should be trying to do lots of things that the editor can have fun with. The editor should be paying attention to what is going on so as not to miss a good opportunity to come in. The narrator should attempt to use all of the tools at his disposal at some point in the scene.

233

Variations

1. Other tools — The same premise can be taken to other forms of narration by changing the tools available: Pop-up book (pop-ups, slides, rotations, repeats, etc.), sports broadcasting, or God influencing the world. **2. Faster and Faster** — This is really a warm-up game. The team performs a scene in ninety seconds and then is required to do it again and again cutting the time by half each time they do it.

Gibberish Interview

Type of Game: Practice Game

Purpose: To use the skills of blind offers and acceptances in a scene-like setting.

Group Size: Three to ten

Duration: About a four-minute scene

Description

Three players sit in a line. The first player is the interviewer. The third player is the expert (who does not speak English) and the second player is the translator. The interviewer asks questions (about a topic obtained from the audience or coach) which are translated into gibberish by the translator. The expert responds in gibberish which is translated again for the interviewer and audience.

Notes

There are a couple of hints to make this game funny. The expert should be as animated as possible. They should almost physicalize the answer. The translator has lots of time to think up an appropriate response, and should not repeat in words what the expert physicalized. It is often entertaining for the translator to say something which contradicts what the expert is "saying." The translator can also act as a blatant "censor." One of the most popular gimmicks in this game is changing the length of answers (The gibberish answer is long and the translation is one word, or the gibberish is very short, but has a very long translation).

Variations

1. **Word at a time expert** — Instead of a gibberish expert and a translator the interviewer is interviewing a panel of three people who speak one word at a time (see the Phrase-at-a-time game).

2. **Gibberish dictionary** — One player says a gibberish word, the next gives the English definition (or the English translation if you prefer). More of a warm-up game to get the mind thinking than anything else. There is no interviewer in this variation.

Limitations

Type of Game: Practice Game (Dealing with limitations)
Purpose: To perform a scene while dealing with some sort of limitation.
Group Size: Two to ten
Duration: About a four-minute scene

Description

The players perform a normal scene but are given limitations that they must abide by. For example:

- Alphabet game and its variations (see the Practice game).
- Players must always sing or rhyme.
- Feet cannot touch the floor.
- One player must have their head in a bucket at all times (more popular than you would think).
- Can only talk when they are touching an object (A good game to force physicalization).
- Only player with the "ball" can talk. After one sentence they must pass the ball.
- Players must touch another player to talk.
- All statements must involve an animal.
- Cannot talk when they are moving, must move whenever they are not talking.

Etc.

Notes

Limitation games are good games to keep "crazy" players under control. When a player steals the focus too often or does not listen to the other players, it is a good time to play a limitation game.

Variations

1. Different strokes, different folks — Each player is given their own unique limitation. **2. A scene without ...** — The scene is performed "without" something. (i.e., a scene without hands or a scene without gravity, etc. **3. Scene in reverse** — A very hard scene. The entire scene is performed in reverse. There are a couple of ways to do it. The cheating way is to "speak backwards," which is basically just gibberish. The hardest way is to do each line of dialog normally, but in a reverse order, for example:

> A: I'm really not interested.
>
> B: But it's really nice.
>
> A: I'm sorry, I would rather walk.
>
> B: Would you like to buy my car?

A final choice is to perform each scene normally, but have each additional scene take place further in the past (like the famous *Seinfeld* episode).

Singing and Rhyming

Improv is constantly changing and improving. One of the recent trends is the use of singing and rhyming in scenes. Teams that have mastered the improv basics may wish to add singing or rhyming to their repertoire.

Why sing or rhyme in an improv scene?

A scene that is done in rhyme shows an extra level of improv skill not seen in other improv games. It is not easy to rhyme off the cuff, at least not without proper training and skill. By making a structure that involves rhyming, teams have increased the difficulty of the scene, and if they can pull off something that another team might not be capable of, it is that much more impressive. This will show itself both in the audience reaction, and if in a competition, in the score.

How can rhyming be added to a scene?

There are a number of places where singing or rhyming can be placed in a scene depending on how many people on the team are capable of rhyming and how skilled they are at it. Here are a number of examples of integrating improvised rhyme into a scene.

- A narrator tells a story in verse while other players on the team act it out. Sometimes these other players say lines of their own — either in verse or just regular speech. Notice that this method is very similar to a one-narrator story structure. In order for one person to carry a scene all the way through like this, they must be an exceptional rhymer.

- The entire team shares the spotlight with each character rhyming or singing whenever they speak. This allows a team to show their depth by revealing that everyone on the team can sing or rhyme. It also takes the burden off one person. While players one and two are speaking, players three and up can be thinking of their next rhymes. Players one and two are not required or expected to keep going through the entire scene, a sometimes intimidating proposition. Broadway musicals are examples of a style where although there are still major players, virtually everyone is singing/rhyming.

- Singing or rhyming works nicely to highlight part of a scene or as a translation from one part of the scene to the next. Some styles (such as children's shows) illustrate the use of song as part of a larger structure. Imagine as well, the use of song as a bridge between changes of location or action — a hero is traveling on a journey with a background song narrating his exploits.

What styles involve singing or rhyming?

Lots of them. One advantage of learning how to improvise songs and rhymes is that it allows you to perform many styles or structures that you could not otherwise have performed (it can also help in other games when players get characteristics like "poetic" or occupations like "opera singer" or "rock star"). Here are some theatrical/media styles that rely heavily or entirely on singing/rhyming:

Opera	Beatnik Poetry
Blues	Rap
Gospel/Church choirs	Medieval
Broadway Musical	Karaoke Bar
Monastic Chant	Children's Theatre
Cultural rituals/festivals	Percussion Drumming
(rhythmic drumming, chanting, etc.)	

When does singing not work?

There are two important instances when singing or rhyming does not help a scene, but actually hurts it. Both instances involve

240

attempts to place singing in a scene when the team is not yet ready.

- **Fake rhymes** — Sometimes when a team decides they want to try singing they do not spend enough time learning the skills. Instead of changing their mind and trying something different they try to "trick" the audience and the judges with fake rhymes. Fake rhymes are rhymes which are not improvised. The easiest way to catch these are to look for cases when the rhymes relate to the structure and not to the suggestion (see Using Your Suggestion, Chapter Four). Examples of these attempts abound, and they are not a good way to do improv.

For example, consider a team which asks for an occupation and a location. They decide to do their scene in verse, and one of their rhymes looks like this:

I had a friend who had a job.
He went to the *location* but he didn't rob.
He used his *occupation* skills
To help girls by the name of Jills.

Notice that any location or occupation could be subbed in and the rhyme would still make sense (and it would still rhyme). This team could do the same scene every time with the same rhymes. There is no skill in "plugging-in" the suggestions in the middle of set rhymes. A better rhyming scheme would be (for the occupation "Scuba-diver" and the location "supermarket"):

My scuba friend was A-OK
When he went to the IGA.
He walked on in with his breathing tank,
Because the food there, it really stank.

Notice that at least one of each rhymed pair: A-OK/IGA and

tank/stank are related to the suggestion. This is what is known as a "real" rhyme.

Even teams which would not consider using "fake-improv" still need to think about the idea of "fake-rhymes." If teams are doing real improv, but the rhyming words they use do not relate to the suggestion, then the audience and the judges do not know they are doing real improv. They cannot tell the difference between the team which improvises rhymes which do not relate to the suggestion and the team which plans all of its rhymes in practice. Players have to prove that they are improvising, and the way to do that is to use the suggestions in the rhymes.

• **No rhymes** — Equally hard to watch is the team which attempts to do a rhyming structure, but does not yet have the ability to do it. They go out and miss rhymes. This is OK every now and then (and can even be endearing if the team presents themselves right), but if players miss more than a few it looks bad. Teams are far better off to present a funny and entertaining scene without rhymes than they are to try to rhyme when they are not yet capable of it. If teams ensure that they can rhyme consistently for an entire practice, then they can be fairly assured of success in a brief performance.

How does an improvisor learn to sing?

There are a number of exercises that will help a player learn how to rhyme and sing. These exercises have been set up in a systematic manner which when followed one after another can teach a team how to rhyme. After becoming skilled at one exercise, teams should move on to the next — teams must be wary of moving through these skills too fast. On the other hand, if players are growing tired with one exercise, trying another for variety could be helpful.

Exercise #1 — Speaking in a beat

In order for rhyming to work it has to be done in proper beat. A vast knowledge of musical theory isn't necessary, but a basic understanding of rhythm is important before any song or rhyme sounds good. The first game to play is the Word Number game. This exercise will teach players to pay attention to the number of words they use in speech. Once players are easily able to count and judge the number of words they use they can try the same game with the variation Syllable Number game. After a comfort level has been achieved, improvisers can add a beat to it. Effectively, a beat is an emphasis placed somewhere in the sentence. For example:

Here we go what *do* you say?
Or,
I *don't* know *how* you feel.

Rearranging the emphasis points in the rhyme's sentence alters the meaning and rhythm. If a team discovers a beat that works really well, it could be used for the remainder of the games in this section. Teams may wish to learn other beats later, but sticking with one at the beginning may simplify the learning process.

Exercise #2 — Learning the good words

Rhyming something with "way" is easier than rhyming something with "orange." When singing or rhyming, players will sometimes have to end a line without knowing what will be said to end the verse. Other times one player may start a line and someone else on the team will finish the rhyme. If a player finishes a line, knowing that a teammate will finish it, the line should be ended on a word which can be easily rhymed.

For this exercise have the group sit in a circle. Choose a syllable with which everyone must end their lines. Proceed around the circle telling a story one line at a time. Each line should end with the desired syllable. Players can even choose what word they will end their line in before the game starts, as long as they are ready to change it if someone else uses it. For example:

ay: way, say, nay, bay, hay, OK, play, may, day ...
ee: free, me, see, gee, flee, plea, key, re-, Eddy ...
i: fly, my, try, die, bye, nigh, why, hi, cry, sly, fry ...

at (ap): mat, cat, drat, fat, hat, map, flap, cap, lap ...
oh: flow, moe, doh!, row, tow, go, so, pro, crow, quid-pro-quo ...
ow (own): how, wow, cow, crown, frown, gown, mee-ow, dow
(jones) ...
aw: draw, saw do-daw, haw-haw, ra, pizza, jaw ...

Note that some syllables can be rhymed with others that are not quite perfect. Consider the rhyme:

I'll go sit down on my mat.
And maybe lie down for a nap.

Mat and nap do not really rhyme, but for the purposes of improvised singing, players can easily get away with it, and often create additional laughs if they rhyme lengthy words with numerous syllables.

Exercise #3 — Learning the good words II

Now that players can get through exercise #2, it is time to mix things up a bit. Using the same basic game, teams should throw in these changes (one at a time):

- Split the group into pairs. Each pair gets one syllable. So pair one might have "ay," pair two "ee" and so on. Now when improvisers tell the story there will be a little more variety.

- Give each individual their own syllable. Each player now does two lines each. For example:

Player 1: I will go to the store today
            To buy all of their hay.
Player 2: And when I get there I will see
            That everything I want is free.

- Now have players choose three or four syllables. Everyone must end their lines in one of these sounds. Obviously the second player of every verse will have to follow the lead of the player before him (so that it stays in rhyme). The next player can then choose any one of the syllables to end their line. For example:

Player 1: The cow ran and jumped with glee
Player 2: Until it fell down on its knee.
Player 3: And then you know it was very bad
Player 4: Before that day the cow was rad.

The next step in this game is giving each player two lines. The first line finishes the rhyme from the player before them and the second line starts a new rhyme for the player after them. For example:

Player 1: Here we go I say to you
Player 2: That I will always see you through
          For until that bright and shiny day
Player 3: When all our friends go out to play
          I'll be with you until the end
Player 4: And we will always be close friends
          But more than that I tell you now ...
Etc.

Exercise #4 — Using the suggestion

Ideally most rhymes in a scene are going to relate to the suggestion. Unfortunately not all words relating to suggestions end in "easy" syllables. This game helps develop the ability to rhyme outside of the structure given in exercises two and three.

When players rhyme a "hard" word that is directly related to the suggestion, they will almost always get a quality laugh. In a rhyming couplet, both ending words don't always need to relate to the suggestion (although it is pretty incredible if done consistently!). If a player has to choose between making the first or second line of a couplet relate to the suggestion, making it the second one will enhance the effectiveness of the punch-line. For example, if the suggestion was "chocolate bars," consider these two couplets:

Trying to get the bar out of the package
Takes an awful lot of wackage.

or,

When I started it took a lot of wackage
to get my chocolate out of the package.

The first option begins with something related to the suggestion and then finishes with a nonsense word. In the second option, the rhyme begins with nonsense, building up anticipation for the second line, which is a clever punchline. The second option is more impressive than the first because the last line in the first option sounds like a player scrambling to finish the rhyme, whereas the second option sounds like a carefully planned joke.

For this game the group leader gives a suggestion (anything will do). The group then has time to individually think of words which are related to the suggestion. Every player should come up with their own word, and they need not be creative, as long as words relate to the suggestion. They then think of another word (any word) which rhymes with their chosen word. After about a minute everyone sings about the suggestion one at a time around the circle. Players should remember to put the related word in the second line of the rhyme.

This game can be expanded upon by giving the players less time and/or making them come up with more than one rhyming verse. Eventually, teams should be able to play this game in a circle going around and around several times. This game could be played in an elimination format where any player missing a rhyme or pausing is eliminated. Seeing who can last the longest indicates the team's top rhymer (important for making selections in rhyming games).

Exercise #5 — Three Topics Game

For this game the team should set up in a symmetric manner facing the same direction (i.e., where the audience will be). With some members sitting in chairs and others standing behind them, they are fairly close together, but all of their faces can be seen. The team will be given three topics to sing about. This game is much more free form than the other rhyming exercises mentioned thus far. Anyone can sing at any time (teamwork is crucial). Using techniques developed in the earlier exercises, the team tries to keep the song going.

The key to making this game work is support. When players are not singing, they should be helping hum/sing/etc., the background melody. For example:

	Player 1: Well I am trapped here in this hole ...
Echoes:	Player 2: Yes, he is trapped there in the hole ...
	Player 1: And I got no place to go
	Player 3: He's trapped and he can't get out ...
	Player 1: What will I do and what will I say
	These things don't happen every day
	Player 4: No, they don't happen every day ...

If players do not help out on their own it may be necessary to assign roles to each person. (Hopefully some balance will occur so that the same people are not singing all the time).

Exercise #6 — Who's next?

Often teams will have one or two players who are much better rhymers than the others on the team and are more confident with their abilities. Sometimes the other team members get intimidated and do not sing when they should. This puts undue pressure on the players who are singing, and the process builds on itself. This game is meant to put a halt to that process.

This game starts the same as exercise #5, only this time there needs to be a leader to run the game. The leader begins the game by pointing at a player. That player sings. After the first player has sung a few lines the leader moves to a new player. This process continues in a somewhat random manner (but making sure everyone has a turn). The leader can stay with one player as long as they like (forcing them to just keep singing), or may just move on after a single line. Note that the leader can change players in the middle of a verse, forcing the new player to finish a rhyme started by someone else (similar to exercise #3).

This game teaches players to think on their feet and always be prepared. They never know when they are going to be called on so they always have to be ready and listening.

Exercise #7 — Putting it in motion

Now that the team is comfortable rhyming, it is time to combine it with their other skills. Have half the team act as narrators and the other half act out the story they tell. Teams could even begin to have some of the "actor" players rhyme their lines while they are acting out the narration (just like the Typewriter game). For variety, have players switch it up and have less or more player narration. Eventually try telling stories without the narrator at all, just everyone rhyming. Teams can play any of the normal games discussed in the Appendix with the addition of a rhyming requirement.

Some other important points

After players have gone through the first few basic exercises they will know *how* to rhyme. The problem is that knowing how to do something and actually doing it are two different things. It is easy to say rhyme this or sing that, but being in front of an audience and attempting to make things work is often quite difficult. The key to success is to have players relax and enjoy themselves.

It is easy to get caught up in self-doubt. Many beginning rhymers become concerned with what is coming up next. They get worried that they will not be able to rhyme a later couplet or that they will not be able to come up with a word that fits into their rhyming scheme. They become too worried about the future and not concerned enough with the present. The key to successful rhyming is to just keep going. It's amazing what the human sub-conscious will come up with if allowed. When players are done, they will be able to look back in amazement that they rhymed *truth* with *uncouth*.

Beginning rhymers should expect to make lots of mistakes. Novices will fumble and lose their beat. Many, many, many rhymes will be missed. Players will get discouraged. No one gets better without practice. If improvisers get frustrated and let other teammates take all the rhymes, then they will never improve. When in a rhyming scene, players must pay attention to the other players and not be afraid to enter a scene. When on stage, it is amazing what magically appears in the mind. With every attempt it will get easier (and the great thing is, it is like riding a bike. Rhymers will be able to do it for the rest of their lives).

If a player is in the spotlight and misses a rhyme, they must not worry. Rhyming is very challenging and very impressive. The audience does not expect each player to make every rhyme. Taking mistakes in stride is essential. Smiling keeps a positive attitude. Smiling at the audience is charming. If a player is standing at the front of the stage singing in beat, having a good time and missing many rhymes, they will still be more entertaining to watch than someone who is visibly terrified about what comes next, even if they make all their rhymes.

Most importantly, all improv skills still hold true in the world of rhyming. (Singing in rhyme is no excuse to block, wimp, or waffle!)

Appendix Five
Lists

A series of lists follows. They can be of some help during practice. We have included lists for most of the common ask-fors (as well as a list of less common ask-fors). Hopefully these lists will show the variety of the suggestion responses that can be received. Use them as you will.

Ask-Fors

Location
Occupation
Ink blot test result
Object
Fairy tale
Characteristic
Goal
Verb
Noun
Limerick
Nursery rhyme
Secret
Character from children's literature
Villain
Movie title
Book title
Emotion
Magazine
Country
Method of transportation
Holiday
Theme
Issue scenario
Belief
Problem
Relationship
Historical event
Physical object from the audience
Animal
Famous person
A day from someone's life
A game show

Method of relaxation
Hobby
Dangerous activity
Injury
Natural event
  (*not* a natural disaster)
Sport
Activity
Place of work
Time period
Room in a house
Television show
Style
Bible story
Food
Obsession
Board game
Sin
Crime
Controversy
Choice
Body part
Super hero
Flaw
Virtue
Reason to take over the world
School subject
Philosophy
Environment (jungle, arctic ...)
Type of container
Unsolved mystery
Significant event in someone's life

Ritual
A myth
Trivia question
A family activity
Something someone could sell
Accident
Horoscope
Famous person
Famous statement (i.e., "Give me liberty
    or give me death")
Newspaper headline
Personal ad
Letter to Dear Abby
Horoscope
TV Guide entry synopsis
Believe it or not entry
Guinness world record
Skill
Area of expertise

Locations

Barbershop
Houseboat
_____ factory
Arctic
Jungle
Eiffel Tower
Statue of Liberty
Parliament Hill
Saloon
Prison
Police station
Fire station
Bedroom
Ocean liner
Titanic
Atlantis
Smurf village
Courtroom
Greenhouse
Taxi Stand
Ballroom
Pool Hall
Bowling alley
Rock concert
Tree house
Circus
Wind tunnel
A big shoe

Swamp
Wonderland
Oz
Bear cave
Basketball court
Sitcom set
Rideau canal
Bull-fighting arena
Stable
Radio station
Lighthouse
Karate dojo
Spaceport
Living room
Spiderweb
Beaver dam
Optometrist's office
Doctor's office
Dentist's office
Bunker
Trench
Desert
Camping tent
Camping site
Backstage
Greenroom
Bus stop
Airport
Airplane
Running track
Sweatshop
Merry-go-round
Sesame Street
Heaven
Hell
The Love Boat
Enchanted forest
Kennel
Travel agency
Niagra Falls
CN Tower
Café
Curling rink
Shooting range
Moon
Super Mario World
Weight room
Car garage
Zoo
Computer lab

251

Bingo hall
Oil rig
Submarine
Pirate ship
Chocolate factory
University
Biology classroom
Stonehenge
Disco bar
Forest
Football arena
Power plant
Castle
Sun
Human heart
Hospital
Cuckoo clock
Picnic park
Jungle-gym/playground
X-men danger room
Swimming pool
Graveyard
Science lab
House of Knives
Careland (home of the Care Bears)
Highway
Pumpkin patch
Purgatory
Postal outlet
Halfway house
Television station
Mansion
Cardboard box
Narnia
Superman's ice palace
Sewer system
Bar
Museum
Big Ben
Clock tower
Fast food restaurant
Mars
Monster truck rally
Lighthouse
Bridge

Genres

Workout video
Cooking show
Gossip column
Entertainment magazine (i.e.,
    Entertainment Tonight, Extra)
Coming-of-age drama (i.e., *The
    Wonder Years*)
Televangelist
Interactive CD-ROM
Music video
Mystery (i.e., Sherlock Holmes,
    Matlock)
Court TV
Sitcom
Ghost story
Romantic comedy
Blues
Beatnik poetry
70s cop show
Medical drama
Adult cartoon satire
Mime
Silent movie
Action movie trailer
Rock opera
Melodrama
Soap opera
Broadway
Instructional manual
Percussion drumming
Fable
Stanley Kubrick film
Science fiction
Heroic fantasy
Infomercial
Saturday morning cartoon
Western
Opera
Piano bar
Teen Magazine
Children's show
Magic show
Theatre of the Absurd
Variety show
B horror film
Gothic horror
Shakespeare
Morality play

Espionage
Web site
Dr. Seuss
Pop-up book
Cultural tale (many possible
   cultures)
Nature documentary
Safety video
Bible story
Cyber-punk — Dark Future
Distopian Literature
Cheesy 60s action show
    (i.e., *Batman, Wonder Woman,*
    Green Hornet)
Clown
Mask
Nihilist theatre
Documentary
Musical
Special interests show
Radio play
Commedia del'arte
Quentin Tarantino film
Bertolt Brecht theatre
Samuel Beckett theatre
Steinbeck
Motivational speaker

Concepts (Themes)

Reactions
Gatherings
Rituals
Memory
Music
Chaos
Risk
Solutions
Impulses
Information
Traditions
Freedom
Prosperity
Prevention
Destinations
Links
Courage
Distance
Messages

Order
Law
Crime
Power
Commerce
Wants
Science
Language
Disasters
Supernatural
Movement
Alterations
Music
Proofs
Relationships
Exploration
Speed
Markings
Signs
Clues
Evolution
Ideas
Hardships
Harmony
Wisdom
Death
Opposites
Changes
Emotions
Entertainment
Transportation
Needs
Fame
Consequences
Hope
Pressure
Chances
Fate
Energy
Danger
Experience
Authority
Beliefs
Industry
Patterns
Connections
Power
Education
Learning
Fantasy

253

Logic
Time
Aging
Secrets
Control
The Future
Differences
Peace
Commitment
Cooperation
Celebration
Progress
Motivation
Preferences
Conflict
Pride
Perseverance
Youth
Technology
Light
Crime
Order
Opposites
Friendship
Joy
Patriotism
Improvement
Flexibility
Desperation
Revenge
Honor
Intelligence
Observation
Mercy
Attractions
Limits
Loss
Necessities
Justice
Survival
Twists
Knowledge
Adventure
Comfort
Philosophy
Beauty
Stress
Discoveries
Creation
Nature

Excess
Motion
Destiny
Perfection
Predictions
Ideas
Leadership
Style
Paranoia
Life
Trade-offs
Art
Images
Purpose
Promises
Ideals
Games
Intelligence
Conflict
Dreams
Personalities
Experience
Authority
Priorities
Environment
Patterns
Effort
Skill
Mystery
Economics
History
Options
Communication
Lies
Control
Tradition
News
Politics
Endings
Obstacles
Beginnings
Accidents
Advice
History
Villains
Heroes
Supernatural
Priorities
Corrections
Danger

Feelings
Identity
Fashion
Trends
Markings
Transformations
Distortion
Avoidance
Abundance
Accessories
Technology
Community
Adjustments
Unity
Perseverance
Rights
Trends
Goals
Peace
Aging
Fears
The future
Creations
Health
Demands
Discoveries
Poetry
Leisure
Learning
Family
Expressions
Accomplishments
Entertainment
Comedy
Pride
Prejudice
Decisions
Delusions
Routines
Firsts
Adventure
Values
Rules
Power
Status
Innovation
Identity
Growth
Progress
Possessions

Characteristics

Approachable
Argumentative
Arrogant
Absent-minded
Academic
Affectionate
Aggressive
Agreeable
Ambitious
Angelic
Angry
Angst-ridden
Animalistic
Annoying
Apathetic
Artificial
Artistic
Athletic
Authoritarian
Awkward
Bitter
Bizarre
Belligerent
Brave
Brilliant
Boring
Bureaucratic
Calculating
Callous
Calm
Carefree
Careful
Casual
Charismatic
Cheerful
Clever
Clumsy
Cocky
Cold
Confident
Confused
Conniving
Considerate
Controlling
Cool
Courageous
Courteous
Cowardly

Crabby
Crafty
Crazy
Critical
Creative
Crude
Cruel
Cunning
Curious
Curt
Daring
Defensive
Depressed
Demanding
Destructive
Devious
Diplomatic
Dirty
Disgusting
Dishonest
Disorganized
Disruptive
Dominating
Dry
Dull
Eager
Easily amused
Egotistical
Enchanting
Energetic
Entertaining
Enthusiastic
Ethical
Extroverted
Faithful
Famous
Fearful
Flamboyant
Flirtatious
Forgetful
Formal
Frank
Frivolous
Frustrated
Friendly
Furious
Generous
Gentle
Giving
Glamorous

Gothic
Graceful
Gracious
Greedy
Grouchy
Gullible
Happy
Hateful
Heroic
Hesitant
High-culture
Hip
Honorable
Hostile
Hot-headed
Humane
Humble
Hyperactive
Hypnotic
Hypochondriac
Ignorant
Ill-tempered
Impatient
Imaginative
Immature
Impulsive
Incompetent
Inconsiderate
Independent
Indecisive
Industrious
Inept
Infantile
Ingenious
Insensitive
Intelligent
Introspective
Introverted
Inventive
Impatient
Irritable
Jealous
Jittery
Joyous
Jumpy
Keen
Kind
Laid-back
Lazy
Lethargic

Level-headed
Liar
Lively
Long-winded
Loud
Love-struck
Macho
Majestic
Martyr
Mature
Mean
Meditative
Megalomaniac
Messy
Methodical
Militant
Militarist
Mischievous
Miserable
Miserly
Modest
Moody
Morbid
Mouthy
Narcissistic
Nasty
Naive
Neat
Negative
Nervous
Noble
Nonchalant
Nosy
Noisy
Obedient
Obnoxious
Observant
Oppressive
Optimistic
Organized
Outgoing
Outrageous
Outspoken
Overbearing
Panicky
Pacifist
Passive
Patient
Patriotic
Paranoid

Passionate
Peaceful
Peculiar
Pensive
Perfectionist
Pessimistic
Picky
Poetic
Polite
Political
Politically correct
Practical
Predictable
Presumptuous
Primal
Prissy
Procrastinator
Proud
Provocative
Psychic
Psychotic
Pushy
Quiet
Quick-tempered
Rebellious
Relaxed
Reserved
Retiring
Romantic
Rough
Rude
Ruthless
Sacrificial
Sad
Sadistic
Sarcastic
Skeptical
Scheming
Scholarly
Secretive
Sensitive
Shallow
Shy
Self-centered
Selfish
Senile
Sensual
Serious
Sexy
Sharp

Shrewd
Silly
Sincere
Sleazy
Sloppy
Smart
Smug
Sneaky
Snobby
Spontaneous
Stressed
Studious
Submissive
Suicidal
Suspicious
Sympathetic
Tactful
Talkative
Temperamental
Thick-skinned
Thoughtful
Thoughtless
Thrifty
Timid
Tortured
Tough
Traitorous
Trustworthy
Truthful
Tyrannical
Uncaring
Unfriendly
Underhanded
Unstable
Unusual
Unreliable
Warm-hearted
Weak-willed
Whiny
Weird
Vain
Verbose
Vile
Violent
Wacky
Wishful
Wishy-washy
Worrisome
Xenophobic
Zealous

Occupations

Business/Politics
Lawyer
Judge
President
Politican
Diplomat
Lobbyist
Union activist
Mayor
Accountant
Contractor
Architect
Economist
Insurance broker
Banker
Marketing director
Secretary
Dictator
Real estate agent
Quality control technician
Union boss
Consultant
Negotiator
Royalty
Salesman
Member of parliament
Manager

Sports
Archer
Referee
Umpire
Coach
Cyclist
Karate instructor
Parachutist
Race car driver
Pro wrestler
Football player
Hockey player
Basketball player
Soccer player
Sports agent
Boxer
Exercise instructor
Tennis star
Snowboarder
Surfer

Performance
Singer
Dancer
Stand-up comic
Photographer
Writer
Lounge singer
Mime
Cartoonist
Movie critic
Radio DJ
Organist
Actor
Ballerina
Weatherman
News anchor
Talk show host
Film man
Director
Make-up artist
Hypnotist
Magician
Illusionist
Opera singer
Poet
Playwright
Clown
Artist
Movie star
Rodeo clown
Advice columnist
Astrologer
Novelist
Escape artist
Music video director
Rock star
Ringmaster

Plants/Animals
Logger
Lumberjack
Farmer
Animal trainer
Safari guide
Exterminator
Fisherman
Zookeeper
Dog handler
Tree planter
Tree farmer

Lion tamer
Shepherd

Military/Police/Crime
Criminal
Warden
Guard
Policeman
Sheriff
Demolitions man
Mafia don
Bouncer
Fireman
Ambulance driver
Border guard
Super hero
Soldier
Bodyguard
Submarine commander
Detective
Assassin
Pirate
Spy
SWAT team member
Drill sergeant
Serial killer
Knight
Criminal
Mastermind
Metermaid
Traffic cop

Retail
Florist
Tailor
Cobbler
Hot dog vendor
Baker
Convenience store worker
Jeweler
Butcher
Candlemaker
Chocolate maker
Donut store employee
Attendant
Gas station worker
Pawn broker
Gunsmith

Science/Academia

Cartographer
Zookeeper
Teacher
Statistician
Mathematician
Chiropractor
Astronaut
Doctor
Opthamologist
Psychologist
Psychiatrist
Engineer
Principal
Historian
Professor
Biologist
Librarian
Pharmacist
Computer programmer
Chemist
Scientist
Brain surgeon
Physiotherapist
Geneticist
Dentist
Archeologist
Paleontologist
Botanist
Chess master
Philosopher
Inventor
Meteorologist
Architect
Museum curator

Other

Sailor
Mountain climber
Fairy godmother
Helicopter pilot
Bandleader
Scuba diver
Airplane pilot
Con man
Blood donor
Bull fighter
Medic
Spelunker

Service Industry

Priest
Taxi driver
Pizza delivery guy
Locksmith
TV repairman
Plumber
Flight attendant
Babysitter
Carnival worker
Cable guy
Bartender
Painter
Masseuse
Courier
Toy maker
Window cleaner
Astrologist
Travel agent
Waitress/waiter
Tour guide
Janitor
Mechanic
Electrician
Translator
Gravedigger
Mortician
Interior decorator
Hairstylist
Cook
Garbage man
Construction worker
Rabbi
Railway engineer
Bus driver
Truck driver
Pool cleaner
Assembly line worker
Midwife
Restaurateur
Telephone operator
Caterer
Squeegy kid
Handyman

Scenarios (both silly and sincere)

- A teenager arrives home past his/her curfew.
- Your teacher has ESP.
- A person has failed to achieve a goal.
- A natural disaster is about to strike.
- There is a reunion between long-lost friends or family members.
- A child has fallen inside a well.
- A group of oddly-dressed people come to your door. It is not Halloween.
- Your pet has grown 100 times bigger than it used to be.
- Your family is moving far away.
- You have won the lottery.
- You are a twin. You have planned a surprise party for your twin. Your twin has planned a surprise party for you at the same time.
- One morning the sun does not rise.
- Your demanding boss has given you an unrealistic ultimatum.
- You have shrunk to five centimeters high.
- Your car has been stolen.
- You catch an intruder in your house — he was your childhood mentor.
- You run a construction firm. You have just finished building a house when you discover some important beams in your van (rather than in the house where they belong).
- You are a surgeon who has just sewn up a patient. You cannot find your watch.
- Upon waking in the morning, you notice that your skin is blue.
- A dilemma is forcing you to choose between people you care about.
- You are on the way to a concert. You have lost your tickets.
- It is a couple's first year anniversary. They have each bought the other an unwanted gift.
- People cannot stop playing pranks on you — it is not April Fool's Day.
- A child has asked for an impossible-to-attain present.

- As a child, you were taking a flight. The plane went down in a marsh and you were the only survivor. You have been raised by geese.
- The right and left sides of your body have separate desires.
- Computers take over the world.
- You are being pressured into something you are not comfortable with.
- You are very hungry. You are made of ice cream.
- An encounter with a celebrity proves to be an interesting experience.
- An infant has accidentally destroyed something of incredible value.
- You are at a sports stadium cheering on the visiting team.
- A change in appearance has changed other people's perceptions of you.
- A child asks you a question you have trouble answering.
- You took a chance that did not pay off.
- You discover the tooth fairy is real.
- There is a lack of trust.
- Someone you know claims to be Little Red Riding Hood.
- It's time you told the truth.
- A deadline is fast approaching.
- You trusted someone to do something important and they did not follow through.
- You have a change of heart.
- Your passion for an activity has decreased.
- Everything has come to a head at once.
- Your reputation precedes you.
- You are breaking up at an inopportune time.
- You are turning into a cat, but your family does not believe you.
- Your vacation is not what you expected.
- You have been refused acceptance into something you did not want, but thought you would get anyway.
- You got something your friend really wanted. They did not get it.
- People are shocked at how you have changed.
- An incidental experience has changed your life.

- It was your last chance, but you still failed.
- You have mixed-up priorities.
- You have been given powers beyond your control.
- The increase of competition has become overwhelming.
- Video games have become more than just that.
- A love from the past has returned at a bad time.
- Someone has assumed you feel the same way they do.
- The gamble did not pay off.
- You have become invisible and mute.
- Time is moving twice as fast for you and everyone around you.
- You have committed yourself to something you always wanted, now you are tempted by something else.
- You have never noticed something incredible right before your eyes.
- It's the first day of school and you are not fitting in.
- You are trying to change for the better.
- What was good in small doses is not so good in extremes.
- You have found a talent you never knew you had.
- You have reached your peak and do not know what to do next.
- You have to choose between two things equally important to you.
- No matter what you do, someone will be hurt.
- Everything you touch turns to gold.
- You found out something important, but no one believes you.
- You changed yourself to fit in, but everyone else changed in a different way.
- What you did affected a large number of people.
- You are trapped in an uncomfortable situation.
- You can see the future, but you cannot change it.
- Everything you write becomes true.
- You came up with and idea on your own. Everyone thinks you copied it.
- You did something wrong and got away with it. Your friend got caught.
- You wake up and cannot remember any of the events in your life.
- Something you never thought would happen happens.

Recommended Reading

This manual aims to introduce improvisation, as well as the techniques needed to develop advanced skills — all in one stand-alone format. Nevertheless, there have been a lot of books written on improvisation before now. Just as watching more improvisation shows will improve a team's ability, so too will reading the opinions and advise of other professionals. We have chosen to describe a few of the better improvisational books on the market. We recommend reading these works before searching for others. For those still interested in the subject, we have compiled a list of other titles which a dedicated researcher may be able to find.

Keith Johnstone
Impro
Considered by some to be "the" book on improvisation. Keith Johnstone founded the Loose Moose Theatre Company, and originated Theatresports. This book delves into the theory behind improvisation. The book is written very academically and you will have to search if you want to find a particular element. The most important aspect explored in this text is the concept of *status*. It is an idea that is very useful in many improvisation scenes and unique to the book.

Keith Johnstone
Impro for Storytellers — Theatresports for Teachers
This is a more practical manual on Theatresports and improv. The most valuable part of the book contains a firm discussion of common "improv problems." It is written very informally, and the advice Johnstone gives is very useful. Other parts of the book detail common Theatresports games and describes how to set up your own tournament.

Viola Spolin
Improvisation for the Theatre

Viola Spolin is considered by many to be the "mother" of improvisation. Her philosophy of using improvisation to help the actor is well utilized by Second City which her son helped to create. Her ideas are presented very differently from Keith Johnstone's. Her work is much respected for working with younger children.

Viola Spolin
Theatre Games for the Classroom

This is a collection of games that can be used in an improv practice. There is a wide range, and many are suitable for players who are not ready for the material presented in *The Ultimate Improv Book*

Kathleen Foreman and Clem Martini
Something Like A Drug - An Oral History of Theatresports

For those interested in the history of improvisation, this book has it all. It shows how Theatresports-style improv first developed and grew to be the huge force it is today.

Philip Bernardi
Improvisational Starters

If you liked our lists you will love this book. It is page after page of lists and scenarios you can use in your rehearsals. No theory or discussion at all.

Charna Halpern, Del Close and Kim "Howard" Johnson
Truth in Comedy

This is the first improv book to specifically discuss "long form" improv. It is a detailed discussion of a performance format known as "the Harold." Any performer who is thinking of creating long (20-40 minute) improv scenes shows should sit down and read this book at some point before you begin.

A Glossary of Improv Terms

These are improvisation terms that are used either specifically in this manual or in the larger improvisational community. Some terms have no known origins and others were created by specific individuals. Any terms that were not specifically created by the authors are commonly used in improv.

Accepting	Taking the offer you are given by another player and using it to further the scene.
Advancing	Moving the scene forward. Doing something new that makes sense with respect to the context of the current scene.
Adjudication	What takes place when an experienced improviser talks to a group after their performance about what went right and what went wrong with their show. Sometimes performed by a coach, other times by an outside source.
Ask-for	Something the team requests from the audience with which to create their scene. It should change either the Who, What, Where, When, Why, or How of a scene. (see Suggestion).
Asking Questions	Making another player define something or make a decision instead of making it yourself. A form of wimping. (see Wimping).
Aside	Takes place when a player exits the scene to talk directly to the audience. It is usually very short. A longer aside is called a monolog or soliloquy.
Background (1)	Anything that is happening apart from the main action of the scene. The physicalization and miming which help to define the location.

Background (2)	The players who are not in the main action. They may enter as walk-ons or accept offers from the main players, but in general they physicalize the location and give focus to the others.
Blind Offer	An offer made wherein the creator of the offer does not know where it will be taken (see Offer).
Blocking	The opposite of accepting. Rejecting or denying an offer and stopping a scene from advancing.
Breaking the routine	Changing the action by doing something related to the original routine. (see Routine).
Cancelling	Accepting an offer and then dropping it from use. Otherwise known as delayed blocking. (See Blocking, Accepting).
Combining	Taking two or more suggestions and using them together in an inter-mixed way. Should take place anytime the team takes two or more suggestions.
Conflict	The basis of most stories. What takes place when the Who encounters the obstacle as they are trying to reach their goal.
Context	The background to which the presentation is taking place. The context of the suggestion is what was asked for. For instance, what is done with the suggestion "banana" should depend on the context (did the team ask for an object or did they ask for a fruit?)
Defining	Identifying characters, objects, places, and so forth in the scene as early as possible.
Denial	See Blocking.
Driving (1)	Being responsible for advancing a scene.
Driving (2)	Taking control of a scene and not letting other players contribute.

Endowing	Giving the location or another player a characteristic based on your actions towards them or it.
Extending (1)	Drawing something out to make it the focus of a scene.
Extending (2)	Drawing something out and delaying instead of thinking of a new idea.
Feeding (1)	Entering the scene from the background and showing the suggestion being used in a new way.
Feeding (2)	Doing something to show someone else's character, or giving them an easy opening to allow their character to be shown in a new way.
Flag	A pre-planned element in a scene that helps the team to use the suggestion.
Focus	The most important thing happening in the scene at the time and where the audience's attentions should be located.
Fill-in-the-blanks	A scene that is not really improvised and only does lip service to the suggestion.
Gagging	Trying to make a joke or do something funny that doesn't flow naturally from the scene. Always a bad idea.
Gibberish	A made-up nonsense language that is used in some games.
Goal	What the player or character is trying to achieve in a scene.
Gossip	Talking about things in a scene instead of doing things.
Handle	Another name for the premise of a scene or structure that is to be done. Usually more general than a structure.

Hedging	A type of delaying. The player waits and spends too much time on something while they think of something else to do.
Hogging	Taking away the focus from the other players and driving the scene on your own.
Huddle	The time a team spends after they get their suggestion for a scene and before they perform the scene. Best to be kept very short (10-30 seconds) so that the audience is not waiting. Some types of improv have huddles as long as 30 minutes.
Instant stakes	Jumping into the action right away without first creating a platform.
Instant trouble	See Instant stakes.
Intro	The preamble to a scene before the suggestions are obtained. The team explains any pre-planned elements that they are going to use in the next scene.
Lip Service (1)	Mentioning the suggestion without really using it in the scene, or having the scene's structure change very little regardless of the suggestion.
Lip Service (2)	Saying the suggestion as a word instead of showing it being used.
Main Player(s)	The players in a particular scene who have the major speaking roles. They should have the focus of the audience's attention through most of the scene.
Mugging	Showing your entire face to the audience and using your facial expressions.
Naming	See Defining.
Narrative	The What. The story that is being told. Most have a clear beginning, middle, and end.

Object (or Objective) See Goal.

Obstacle What is preventing the player or character from directly achieving their goal and ending the scene.

Offer An idea that is presented in a scene by one player that other players can choose to accept or reject.

Physicalization Creating a location or object with mime or body position.

Platform The starting point of a good story. The rest of the scene moves on from the platform. It should take place in a safe, stable environment. (see Routine).

Player An improvisational performer.

Pre-Show What a team does to get ready and pumped up for the show they are about to do.

Raising the stakes Causing more trouble for the main character. Very entertaining for the audience.

Reincorporation Bring back something which happened earlier in the scene.

About the Authors

Edward J. Nevraumont

Edward began improvising with the Canadian Improv Games while in high school. Since then his improv scope has broadened considerably. He has worked in improvised dinner theatre, coached a high school improv team for six years, created the Kingston Improv Games, developed training materials, and facilitated events for drama teachers across Canada. He has studied many different improv schools of thought and worked with everyone from Keith Johnstone to Paul Sills, from Garry Austin to Michael Gellman. He has written training materials for utilizing improvisation in the business world for Queen's University School of Industrial Relations. Currently Edward is using his improvisation techniques as a manager with Procter and Gamble and as one of three directors of "Improv Toronto." (www.improvtoronto.com).

Nicholas P. Hanson

A graduate of the Queen's University Department of Drama, Nicholas teaches improv workshops in schools, universities, summer camps, and workshop settings. As General Manager of the Kingston Improv Games, a high school improv festival, Nicholas has served as a trainer, administrator, judge, adjudicator, host, and late-night problem solver. In his work as an actor, director, and designer of community theatre projects, Nicholas relies on improvisational techniques as an alternative to traditional processes. Currently, Nicholas is adapting his improv curriculum for implementation in social organizations as a means of conflict resolution and societal awareness.

Kurt Smeaton

Kurt is a professional actor/writer, based in Toronto. A graduate of the George Brown Theatre School, Kurt is a former regional and national champion with the Canadian Improv Games. He has judged, trained, and adjudicated improv across Ontario, and was a founding member of an Ottawa-based sketch troupe: The Pez

Family. Kurt has worked extensively in the theatre, performing with such renowned companies as Soulpepper, Theatre Direct Canada, and Actors' Repertory Company. He is currently using his improv skills writing and performing in a number of comedy pilots for television.

Order Form

Meriwether Publishing Ltd.
PO Box 7710
Colorado Springs CO 80933-7710
Phone: 800-937-5297   Fax: 719-594-9916
Website: www.meriwetherpublishing.com

Please send me the following books:

_____ **The Ultimate Improv Book   #BK-B248**   **$16.95**
by Edward J. Nevraumont, Nicholas P. Hanson and Kurt Smeaton
A complete guide to comedy improvisation

_____ **Truth in Comedy #BK-B164**   **$17.95**
by Charna Halpern, Del Close and Kim "Howard" Johnson
The manual of improvisation

_____ **Acting Games — Improvisations and**   **$16.95**
Exercises   #BK-B168
by Marsh Cassady
A textbook of theatre games and improvisations

_____ **Improve With Improv!   #BK-B160**   **$14.95**
by Brie Jones
A guide to improvisation and character development

_____ **Comedy Improvisation   #BK-B175**   **$14.95**
by Delton T. Horn
Improv structures and exercises for actors

_____ **Improvisations in Creative Drama   #BK-B138**   **$15.95**
by Betty Keller
A collection of improvisational exercises and sketches for acting students

_____ **Spontaneous Performance #BK-B239**   **$15.95**
by Marsh Cassady
Acting through improv

These and other fine Meriwether Publishing books are available at your local bookstore or direct from the publisher. Prices subject to change without notice. Check our website or call for current prices.

Name: _____

Organization name: _____

Address: _____

City: _____ State: _____

Zip: _____ Phone: _____
  ❏ **Check enclosed**
  ❏ **Visa / MasterCard / Discover #** _____

Signature: _____   *Expiration date:* _____ _____
        (required for credit card orders)

Colorado residents: Please add 3% sales tax.
Shipping: Include $2.75 for the first book and 50¢ for each additional book ordered.

  ❏ *Please send me a copy of your complete catalog of books and plays.*